The Best Places to Kiss in Paris

Thierry **Soufflard**

adapted by David W. **Cox**

PARIGRAMME

Special Thanks

Great big thank-you kisses to all those who helped
make this guide possible, particularly Sandrine Moreau,
Emmanuelle Stroesser, Sarah Finger, Frédéric Olivier
Boulay, Arnaud Briquet, Laurence Pasquini, Pierre Franchot.
Thanks also to Murielle Carpentier of the Vidéothèque de Paris.

Collection managed by Jean-Christophe Napias

Contributor: Pascal Tilche

Special thanks to Gyoza Media for permission to use their texts.

For
Annabelle,
Annie,
Betty the Sow, Birgit, Caro,
Corinne "the dream",
Danielle, Emma, Eva,
Fernande (oohh Fernande),
Françoise,
Fred,
My beautiful Hélène,
Isabelle,
Laure,
Marie, Marianne, Maya,
Mom,
Grandma Clo-clo, Grandma Giselle,
Nathalie,
Natacha,
Nini Peau d'chien,
Papa,
Lolo, Lolo No. 2, Lolo No. 3,
Patricia,
Petulla "the tart,"
Sandrine,
Sarah,
Sissi (who never ever said "no")
Stéphanie,
Valérie,
Véronique and her magic lipstick,
Virginie,
Yaëlle,
Zora "the redhead"

And their lips oh so sweet...

Reader Beware!
(read this notice carefully)

Warning: The Psychology Department at Western State College in Gunnison, Colorado has stated that "a kiss shortens life by three minutes." A kiss can cause heart palpitations to such a degree that it works harder in four seconds than it normally would in three minutes. According to statistics, 480 kisses will shorten a person's life by one day, 2,360 kisses will cost you a week, and 148,071 kisses... means "quite simply a whole year lost," explains the writer Paul Morand. In other words, if you're concerned about living as long as possible, stop reading this right now!

To those of you who are fond of deadly kisses, welcome, and my apologies for inviting you to end your life a little sooner. But this is to inform those of you who will be consuming this product not to complain about it afterward, because then it will be too late! It's not my position to recommend a moderate or immoderate use of this guide. Rather, as a gentleman, I decline to take any responsibility in regard to romantic problems that might ensue.

Table of Contents

Rationale for this guide

The capital's most delectable sites have not been treated as a subject until now. This guide will attempt to compensate for this unfortunate oversight, which has made it very difficult for Pont-Neuf lovers and lovers elsewhere.

Kissing in public is rare; it simply is not done much anymore. We have become modest, our relationships contractual, and passion is hidden behind closed doors. My goodness, let your kisses be seen on balconies and in the streets! Show your affection. Shout your love from the rooftops of Paris! Do it for others; discover a fresh new flowering of passionate kisses and smiling lips.

Nevertheless, some of you are no doubt mumbling, "What do we need a guide like this for?" True enough, you can kiss anywhere. And since those engaged in kissing are often blind to their surroundings, what does the environment matter? And why choose one location instead of another? But the surroundings can greatly affect the savor and success of a kiss, and therefore nothing can be taken for granted.

Who is this guide for?

It's for those over 77 that love sometimes leaves gaga, and young ones of seven who have probably already experienced their first kiss on the lips. And it's for all young people of in-between years with plans for forthright kisses and loving embraces. So let's go out onto the street and find the places where lovers have left their mark while practicing this exquisite Parisian art.

Introduction: Paris, City of Romance

Paris puts a twinkle in the eyes of lovers the world over because in Paris kissing is... simply marvelous. Like a precious little gem in a romantic jewel box, Paris has always enjoyed this reputation. The roguish François Villon was already proclaiming its merits and attractions in the 15th century. Montaigne literally fell in love with it and wrote: "Paris has possessed my heart since childhood. The more I see of other beautiful cities, the more her beauty claims my affection. I love her for what she is, and more for her simple essence than when she is burdened with the trappings of worldly pomp. I love her tenderly, even her warts and stains."

Throughout the centuries, much ink has been spilled in praise of Paris. The well of ink has not gone dry, nor the "saliva" for that matter. Madeleine de Scudéry asked herself in *The Grand Cyrus*: "Is this where all the ladies at evening in their small open carriages go? And where all the gentlemen on horse do follow? And so, weaving from one dame and then to another, it is both promenade and conversation. Can there be anything else quite so pleasant?" Dorante gushed: "Paris in my opinion is like a storybook land." Likewise Eustache Deschamps, on the evening before leaving the capital, declared his love for his cherished city in *Farewells to Paris*: "Adieu m' love, good-bye sweet young things. Farewell great bridge, food markets, and steam baths. Farewell fine lace, and... fair bosoms."

But, frankly, this is no time for farewells. On the contrary, it is time to set out and discover secret gardens, charming metro stations, and romantic candlelit tables. Onward-ho!

The symbols in this guidebook indicate the following information:

☺ *The most romantic time*
The most romantic season: ✿ *Spring*   ✿ *Summer*
                                  ✿ *Autumn*   ❄ *Winter*
♡ *Long kisses are no problem!*
♥ *Discreet kisses only*

1

The Great Classics

W hat is the first reflex of a couple in love on a visit to Paris? To stroll hand in hand along the Seine; to kiss each other, at least once, while gazing at the Eiffel Tower or Place de la Concorde, to clutch each other passionately at the top of a Montmartre staircase because they have heard that these are romantic places... But the quays along the Seine stretch for miles, and Montmartre has too many stairs to choose from. So which are the most thrilling benches, walkways, and out-of-the-way hideaways? What is the best time of the year or day? When won't your kisses be interrupted by a throng of tourists? Which lovers of the past have tread where lovers of today now bravely venture?

Courtship under the Pont-Neuf

1st arrondissement

Métro Pont-Neuf

In 1994, fashion designer Kenzo covered the Pont-Neuf with flowers from end to end. Therefore, my young fellow, you can see what a gallant gesture you're going to have to make on the oldest bridge in Paris! Show up with a huge bouquet in hand, stroll with your love to the stairs behind the statue of King Henri IV. The stairs lead down to the Square du Vert-Galant. But if this daring move makes her swoon, never fear, paramedics are on the other bank of the river. Dive on in and swim across for help! Ah, what wouldn't you do for love? Once your heart stops racing, you've caught your breath, and your face has taken on some color, go towards the Place Dauphine (which does not rhyme with "depressing scene," as a Jacques Dutronc song claims). I recommend the upper part of the garden, especially the little stone benches beneath the chestnut trees, facing the steps leading up to the Palace of Justice.

☺ *From 6:30 PM to 9:00 PM*

☘ *In the merry month of May when tulips sway in the wind*

♡ *Go for it, and make it long!*

You can even find oxygen at the Samaritaine

1st arrondissement

Métro Pont-Neuf

If you find yourself gasping for air while on the polluted Rue de Rivoli, dash into the sports section at the Samaritaine department store and grab an oxygen tank. Or perhaps you would simply prefer to take the elevator in Store 2 (facing the Seine) up to the terrace on the 9th floor. Take a good deep breath of fresh air and share it with the lady or gent of your choice. Pure bliss! Even though you are far above the traffic below, don't get carried away and go too far because you're not alone. People can see you. Instead, admire the spectacular panoramic view. There in the heart of the capital, Paris wraps you in its own special embrace. Arm in arm, the two of you finally decide to rejoin the little ants below scurrying back and forth on foot, bicycle, and scooter. But before you get to the ground floor exits, put on the blindfolds if you're broke. The reason: an amazing and very tempting display of the finest jewelry, but pricy-pricy! Nevertheless, if you can't manage to slip out the doors without reaching for your wallet, the next step may be the bridal gift registry!

☺ *Afternoon for the best sunlight*

🎊 *When lilies and wedding gifts bloom*

♥ *Someone is bound to be watching*

A Cozy Hotel on the Rue de la Paix

2nd arrondissement

Métro Opéra

As its name indicates, the Rue de la Paix (literally "Peace Street") is a perfect place for making up if you've had a spat. A little box with a gold ribbon from Cartier's automatically brings down the curtain on any dramatic domestic squabble. But the tiniest pretty bauble means you will first have to go to the bank. It's no different than in Monopoly, you'll have to pass "Go" and collect FF20,000 or your account will be in the red. You'll find the entrance to the BNP Paribas branch on the adorable little Cour Vendôme, behind the square of the same name. Just the spot to place your bet... on seduction. Roll the dice and make your move! Good going! You land on "Chance". Draw the card and come up with a sweet little pearl. Plus, you get to move your pawn to the entrance of the Westminster Hotel at 13, rue de la Paix. It's your lucky day! Thanks to the hotel's charm and your little jewel, you've won a heart—and lost your wallet. But when it comes to love, who's keeping count? Anyway, there's no harm in dreaming!

☼ *When night falls and tiaras glitter behind the display windows*
♨ *When you need something warm and cozy*
♡ *You won't be playing Monopoly again, that's for sure!*

The Widow and her Carnival of Courtiers

3rd arrondissement
Musée Carnavalet
23, rue de Sévigné
Tel. 01 44 59 58 58
Métro Saint-Paul

An appropriately lovely name for the abode of a fair lady! At age 25, Madame de Kernevenoy was widowed when her husband was killed in a duel. She was so beautiful that a long carnival-like procession of courtiers came regularly, providing pleasant company. Her suitors found her awkward name at odds with her exquisite beauty, and so gave her the moniker of "Carnavalet."

Transformed today into a museum of the history of Paris, the widow's home has retained the attractive sobriquet given to her. Since that time, local legend has it that people should enjoy themselves there. In honor of the tradition, it is strongly recommended that you take your flirting into the museum hallways or garden. The important thing is to be discreet, just as the original mistress of the house tried to be. Also, take the opportunity to contemplate the portrait of the daughter of Madame de Sévigné—another resident of the Hôtel Carnavalet—, Madame de Grignan, "the fairest young lady of France," painted by Mignard. The portraits of the greatest romantic authors, rendered by illustrious artists, should also pique your curiosity.

☼ *10:00 AM–5:40 PM. Closed on Mondays*
♨ *Museums are heated in winter!*
♥ *Keep an eye out for the museum attendants!*

A Trip to the Tip of the Island

4th arrondissement

Métro Pont-Marie

On the banks of the Île Saint-Louis, at the end of the Quai de Bourbon, an old tree serves as a refuge for sandpipers and gray wagtails. Wild ducks and water hens also flutter their feathers here. Like the tree, you could remain at the jetty's end for years, where, two by two, lovebirds from the four corners of the Earth gather daily. Stone benches serve as a perch for those constant companions who come to rub beaks. It's peaceful and offers a spectacular view. At night, the street lamp acts as a lighthouse, attracting all manner of long and lingering gazes. A cool place to bill and coo! To get there, go down the steps beneath Pont Louis-Philippe or the Quai de Bourbon.

🕐 *All night long*

✿ *By the light of the moon*

♡ *It's now or never!*

A Vow Made by Two under Pont Marie

4th arrondissement

Métro Pont-Marie

Legend has it that if you make a wish under Pont Marie, also referred to as the "lovers' bridge," it will be granted. But you must not tell your companion what you wished for. You have two ways to go under the bridge: by river (on a *bateau-mouche*, barge, raft, buoy, or whatever type of navigation method you choose) or by street (Voie Georges-Pompidou, doo-doopy-doo!).

🕐 *The legend doesn't say anything about a timetable*

⚡ *Your wish won't be drowned in the madding crowd*

♡ *It's pretty obvious, isn't it?*

City Hall Smooch

4th arrondissement
70, rue de Rivoli
Métro Hôtel-de-Ville

The photograph entitled *The Kiss at the Hôtel de Ville* no doubt evokes Paris' most romantic cliché. But where did Robert Doisneau position himself, with his Leica in hand, in order to capture the lovers who today are the most famous in the world? He was on the sidewalk terrace of the café that then stood opposite City Hall (Hôtel de Ville), 70, rue de Rivoli, simply sitting at a table. Pose for the photo with the iron grille of the metro entrance in the background. Ask anybody strolling by, preferably a camera-clutching Japanese tourist, to join the game of recreating Doisneau's famous smooch-shot.

☺ *Mid-afternoon*
🐜 *For the winter attire just like the lovers in the famous photo*
♡ *Several takes may be required*

The Disarming Charms of the Port de l'Arsenal

4th arrondissement
Métro Bastille

The harbor is frequented by rose-garden enthusiasts, tourists signing up for canal-boat rides, and admirers of riverboats. What do pleasure craft owners do in this canal port off Place de la Bastille? They quietly polish their masts, and occasionally score big time! That is, pretty temptresses who steal across their pontoons, most often wearing sandals and burdened with backpacks. The most audacious pleasure boat owners invite these lovely sirens onboard for a river cruise. As for you, after a romantic kiss beside a docked barge, you can drop your anchor at the Grand Bleu Café. Dive into a pool of citrus juice or savor a sherbet while watching the boats return. The Arsenal's luscious garden offers a wonderful view of the peaceful harbor. All this is only a hop and a skip from the revolutionary Colonne de Juillet on Place de la Bastille.

☺ *Cocktail hour*
�֍ *July, because of the column on Place de la Bastille*
♥ *You can really go overboard here!*

A Deluge of Books

5th arrondissement
Quai Saint-Michel
Métro Saint-Michel

During the first early autumn rains, along the Quai Saint-Michel, you'll find delightful rows of booksellers with feet as soggy as rice-paddy farmers. Daniel Halévy wrote: "One characteristic that farmers and booksellers share is having to put up with awful weather." But don't lovers have to, also? Whether decked out in raincoats or straw hats, in hot weather or cold, wind or hail, they'll forever stroll along the Quai Saint-Michel.

☺ *Early in the morning to avoid the tide of humanity*
❀ *Stock up on reading material (and kisses) for the winter*
♥ *Try to avoid kissing right under their noses!*

Love on the Waterfront

5th arrondissement
Métro Maubert-Mutualité

Underneath the parapets of the booksellers along the Quai de la Tournelle, a gently descending paved path guides your steps toward the little port of la Tournelle (three or four riverboats dock there). A stone bench is shaded by a magnificent tree covered with white and green flowers. The bench is level with the barge called the "Léa" and gaily festooned with greenery. Look up toward the left. A miracle looms in the Paris sky! On a clear day, you can see the petticoats of the monumental statue of Saint Geneviève, patron saint of Paris. That little bench is perfect for lovers whispering sweet nothings.

☺ *Between noon and 2:00 PM*
❀ *Beneath a flurry of pollen*
♡ *Make hay while the sun shines!*

Watch your Skirt on the Passerelle des Arts!

6th arrondissement

Métro Saint-Germain-des-Prés

Singer Georges Brassens immortalized this pedestrian bridge's "sneaky breeze that will blow your skirt above your knees!" No need to be a popular French music hall star, even average Joes can use their kissers to serenade their sweetheart on this famed stage spanning the Seine. But they won't be alone because the Passerelle des Arts is a favorite place for lovers the world over. Occasionally it has the charm of an overcrowded tourist attraction. Its reputation was made long, long ago. You see this in all the messages carved with penknife on the benches and planks: "For you, Nathalie, my girl forever," or "For my little sweetie-pie. I'll love you till I die." Unfortunately, the crush of couples does tend to detract from the charm of the place.

☺ *Avoid sundown, peak time for lovers. Instead, go when church bells chime in the dawn. Listen to them in that beautiful setting while your own "sunshine" gently rocks you back and forth. A sound-and-light show you won't want to miss!*

🎄 *It will be all yours on a chilly winter morn!*

♡ *Just like all the other couples*

Place de Furstenberg

6th arrondissement

Métro Saint-Germain-des-Prés

This could have been a charming and lively little spot if the mayor's office had not removed the bench to prevent the homeless from sleeping on it. Do loiterers and lovers not make good company? Or perhaps the romantic beauty of the surroundings is reserved uniquely for the privileged few? In any case, the result is rather unfortunate because, in spite of the magnificent catalpa tree there, the area is most often deserted, with only a rare passerby. Quite a shame because it's a good place to find respite from the din of traffic. A typically Parisian street lamp, planted right in the middle of the square, stands guard with a romantic glow. When night falls, it reminds lovers from around the world that the spot awaits now and forever. Don't miss the charming Delacroix Museum at 6, Place de Furstenberg, tel. 01 44 41 86 50 (open daily except on Tuesdays).

☺ *Morning time is a fine time*
❀ *Amazingly few tourists even in high season*
♡ *Take your stance standing up*

Sculpt your Kisses with Rodin

7th arrondissement
Musée Rodin
77, rue de Varenne – Tel. 01 44 18 61 10
Métro Varenne

Let's take a moment for a bit of art history. If you're searching for something to delight the eyes and, especially, the lips, discover the kisses of Auguste Rodin. First, that fateful work entitled *The Kiss* will allow you to slip into... the subject right away. Let it be the first step on your pilgrimage to the temple of love. Behold how two hearts, fused into this block of cold white marble, come to life in their scorching, turbulent kiss. Imitate that pose and polish off your first smooch in Rodin's honor.

Continue your practice exercises in front of other sculptures that evoke kisses. You'll be inspired by *Adam and Eve*, *Paolo and Francesca*, and *Eternal Springtime*. On the main floor are *Daphnis and Lyce* in room No. 9 and *The Metamorphoses of Ovid* in No. 10. You will also come across a man holding a woman in his embrace while kissing her neck. On the wall, *Vain Tenderness*, a sculpture executed in bas-relief, suggests a softer embrace.

Even more daring are *The Bacchantes*, *The Fall of Icarus*, and, especially, the *Bon Génie* group. To conclude, assume the pose of the mythic bronze *Romeo and Juliet* from 1902. The balcony provides the essential setting. It overlooks a magnificent garden, the perfect resting place to catch your breath—unless, of course, one kiss is not enough.

☺ *Open daily except on Mondays*
❀ *A sunny autumn day is best*
♡ *Camille Claudel wouldn't have it any other way*

Place de la Concorde and Cours-la-Reine

8th arrondissement

Métro Concorde

The Place de la Concorde is said to be the most beautiful square in the world, so I need not regale you with its charms. But visitors should be made aware that it is the point of departure for the Cours-la-Reine, which was the most popular courtly promenade in Europe during the reign of Louis XVI. Begun by Marie de Médicis, the promenade stretched all the way to the Place de l'Alma as throngs of strollers and cavaliers followed the course of the River Seine. The carriages, with their teams of horses, made the U-turn on what is today the Place du Canada. During the 1860s, it was a favorite place for lovers' rendezvous after leaving theater performances. Merchants who sold jellies and fruits pulled double duty as messengers when love letters were slipped into their hands. And everywhere greetings gushed forth since etiquette required that even strangers should salute each other. But today if you get a notion to revive the spirit of the past, you had better be careful not to get run over by the motorized "carriages" of today. What was once a promenade area is now a busy traffic thoroughfare, so it's best not to wander too far off course. Anyway, to hell with nostalgia since all good things must come to an end. You may as well go drown your sorrows at the oldest musical pavilion in Paris, still standing at the Jardin des Champs-Élysées. (Make a beeline into the gardens from Place de la Concorde.)

☺ *Enjoy strolling aimlessly about until the famed hour when Cinderella's carriage turns back into a pumpkin. After that, retrace the steps of grandees who used to pour out onto the Champs-Élysées, dancing in the lamplight on the traffic circle. Give it a whirl!*

❆ *When snowflakes fall*

♡ *Watch out for the spray from the fountains*

Paris Canals by Bike

10th and 19th arrondissements

Métro République

Here is a great itinerary for cycling romantics. First, warm up your facial muscles on the bench in front of 42, Quai de Jemmapes, where you can lock lips near the canal's lock. Once you've unlocked, take off! Feel a sudden urge? Enjoy a French kiss at the footbridge beside the old customs house. Halt! Do you have any love to declare? Lovers of classic French movies can reenact the scene between Arletty and Louis Jouvet on the Grange-aux-Belles footbridge in front of the Hôtel du Nord, for which the Marcel Carné film was named. After all the emotion and effort, refresh yourself with a cool anisette drink at the legendary Hôtel du Nord bar. Ride your bike up to the Bassin du Combat, and, as you pass under the romantic little bridge, sneak a kiss on the way. Your escape route leads through the Rue de Crimée, with Parc de la Villette visible on the horizon. The crowd applauds your performance as you arrive neck and neck: your wheels—and your lips—pressed together. Continue up the bike trail along the canal towards Meaux via Pantin. Further on, outside the outskirts, the country setting offers you serene hide-aways for cuddle-up time.

☺ *Sundays from 2:00–6:00 PM when many streets are reserved for bikers and pedestrians*
❀ *or* ☼ *For the luscious greenery*
♡ *Keep your tires inflated!*

Spin your Wheels at Trocadéro

16th arrondissement
Métro Trocadéro
From the windswept Trocadéro esplanade, the graceful Eiffel Tower provides the finest backdrop in the world for snapshots. How many hugs and kisses have been immortalized on high-gloss paper with the Iron Lady pointing heavenwards? How much lip gloss has been smudged as lovers pucker up for the camera, oblivious to the whiz of daredevil roller-skaters artfully zigzagging through rows of empty soft-drink cans? Zoom in on those lips!

☺ *Sunset, when the tide of tourists subsides*
📷 *Freeze! Now, smile for the birdie!*
♡ *Kisses are part of the scenery!*

Flights of Fancy: the Stairs of Montmartre

18th arrondissement
30–32, rue des Trois-Frères
Métro Abbesses

While love may give you wings, trudging up the steps to the top of the butte is tough on already breathless lovers. So, for those lacking in stamina—or lovers still lacking wings, the bottom steps are a good second choice, especially the first step between No. 30 and No. 32 on the Rue des Trois-Frères. Itinerant lovers visiting Paris need not worry: a little yellow mailbox has been placed at this very spot, so you can share your most immediate and far-away thoughts at the same time. No one will mind your long passionate kisses. On the contrary, they add to the charm of the place. You literally become part of the scenery. A photographer's delight! So smile for the camera!

☺ *Nighttime*
🕭 *When sweet scents waft through the air of Montmartre*
♡ *Obviously!*

Find a Tiny Place... in Your Heart

20th arrondissement
Métro Buzenval

Two benches, a sidewalk café, a few trees on a tiny square... What could be more delightful for two people in the mood for kissing? This modest but beautiful architectural ensemble is as precious and delicate as wildwood flowers. You'll find this petite square located in the pleasant working-class neighborhood of the 20th arrondissement right where Rue Michel-de-Bourges and Rue des Vignoles merge. The little café bears the strange name of "20th Art." *Bizarre, non?* Could they mean the art of kissing? Come find out for yourselves. This is a place where peacefulness hangs in the air, and laundry from the windows. A great spot for bread and cheese.

☺ *6:00–9:00 PM*
🕭 *When wildwood flowers bloom*
♥ *An old-geezer in the neighborhood keeps a watchful eye out*

The RATP Roadsters
Bus lines 29 and 56

Only two city buses have open-air rear sections. They are the 56 line from Clignancourt to Vincennes, and the 29, originating at the Gare Saint-Lazare and stopping at Porte de Montempoivre. Can't afford a fancy convertible? Buy a ticket and enjoy a ride on one of these cabriolet buses! While they are not as impressive as a cherry-red Firebird, these buses are the tops in hair-in-the-wind urban transport! Don't wait too long, though, because little by little, the Paris transit authority (RATP) is replacing these dear old buses with far less romantic upgrades, and without the slightest hint of regret.

🕐 *Avoid rush hour*
🌣 *Hang onto your hat!*
♡ *You expected that, right?*

2

Out of Sight

Where should fugitive lovers hide? Can they avoid discovery by slipping down an alleyway or into a carriage entrance? Can they seek asylum in the anonymous crowd? Anxious and impatient, biting their lips because of an impossible love, the impetuous couple on the run spends each moment looking for a new hideout. But it's not easy to hide an impossible love! These covert locales, however, will never reveal your secrets. Discretion guaranteed.

Village Saint-Paul

4th arrondissement
Métro Saint-Paul
Constructed on the former royal gardens of King Charles V, the Village Saint-Paul has a slightly antiquated air. After Mass on Sundays, the faithful secondhand dealers congregate there; during the week, though, there are devoted lovers. Curious women gather in groups to gossip on the paved courtyard, along with painters, antique dealers, cabinetmakers, restaurant owners, and gourmets. You'll also find a bench there next to a lamp and three trees, where you can spend an idyllic moment in the heart of the Marais district. To get there take the scenic route that leads to 7, Rue Ave-Maria, or the little byway at 26, Rue des Jardins-Saint-Paul.
☺ *From 11:00 AM till 7:00 PM, except for Tuesday and Wednesday*
🌱 *In a thunderstorm... of passion!*
♡ *Idyllic and peaceful*

Slip through the finest carriage entrances

4th arrondissement
Two (legitimate!) propositions

Impasse Guéménée

28, rue Saint-Antoine
Métro Bastille
If by chance you're walking down the sidewalks of Rue Saint-Antoine and you feel a titillation of the lips, a sudden urge to smooch, try lip-locking in this cul-de-sac. Impasse Guéménée has

a turquoise-colored carriage entrance at No. 6 that's inviting for those in a tender mood. Ditto for its brown-hued neighbor, cleverly crowned by a sculpted hat. In a heartbeat, you'll find yourself in front of the charming door to No. 5.

🕐 *Late morning*

🍄 *No shelter in a storm*

♥ *The camera above one of the doors could be spying on you*

Rue Chanoinesse

Métro Cité or RER station Saint-Michel – Notre-Dame

In the shade of the stone skirts of Notre-Dame, Rue Chanoinesse welcomes you with open arms. The carved wooden door at No. 12 waits for passersby to gaze on it and linger a while. At No. 17, set a bit back from the street, is a blue doorway with a charming paved entrance, and a bush there serves discreetly as a screen so you can avoid unwanted encounters. No. 4, the prettiest doorway in Paris without a doubt: coils of wisteria unfurl in a floral carpet onto the sidewalk and part of the street.

🕐 *Late afternoon*

🍄 *Positively!*

♡ *Even if you have bad breath, the scent of flowers will cover up your handicap!*

Behind the Church…

5th arrondissement
Cloître Saint-Séverin
Métro Saint-Michel

There's no chance anyone will discover you here since the entrance to this terrestrial paradise is guarded by… the church. You will need a guide to get in. Oh, but not so quickly! Patience, my dears. You will have to wait until Sunday afternoon rolls round. The church bells will let you know when you can enter. The only way to cross the veil into this magical spot is through Saint-Séverin Church.

Enter through the heavy door on the Rue des Prêtres-Saint-Séverin side, take the hand of your partner in adventure, and don't let go. It's downright spooky! If you bear to the right, you will notice a smaller door. There, grinning gargoyles welcome you as you open it. They keep watch over the comings and goings in this former charnel house (bones of the dead were placed here before the reign of Louis XIII). But don't run off! Because today the "paradise" is a splendid cloister with lovely benches in the shade of two giant chestnut trees. The courtyard is a peaceful and out of the way place. No pedestrians in the street will be able to spy on you here. Nevertheless, be as discreet as your surroundings, otherwise this little piece of heaven might be permanently off limits.

☉ *Sunday afternoons before 5:00 PM*

☼ *A remote spot where you can cook up something for the summer, protected from the tourists...*

♥ *The gargoyles are watching*

Mouth-to-Mouth at the Bottom of the Pool

5th arrondissement
Latin Quarter swimming pool
19, rue de Pontoise
Métro Maubert-Mutualité

The bottom of the sumptuous Latin Quarter pool guarantees a silence that couldn't be more profound (8½ feet deep, to be exact)! Like treasure sunk to the bottom of a lagoon, your kisses will remain a secret, except for the telltale air bubbles... When you come back to the surface (underwater kisses never last very long), you will succumb to the architectural charm. Bath boys still take care of the first-floor changing rooms overlooking the pool. A number of film directors have used this pool for romantic scenes. A scene in the film *Blue*, directed by Krzysztof Kieslowski, was shot here. Emmanuelle Béart splashed in the crystal-clear water here for the Claude Sautet film *Nelly et Monsieur Arnaud*.

☉ *Nightly from 9:00 to midnight. Soft light and mood music. More couples during these hours.*

☰ *From January to March, fewer swimmers means greater privacy!*

♡ *Hold your breath!*

A Resting Place for the Heart

6th arrondissement

Rue Gît-le-Cœur

Métro Saint-Michel

Ci-gît le cœur! is French for "The heart rests here!" A perfect street name for kissing! It was derived from the name of the chef Gilles le Queux. So, it's up to you, chefs of the heart, to get something cooking on the doorstep at No. 10, and mix it carefully (the ingredients, that is). Just past this appetizing entrance, Rue de l'Hirondelle leads you to heavenly enchantments. At the end of the street you'll find a typical Parisian staircase that leads to a ravishing passageway, which, in turn, takes you onto the Place Saint-Michel. At No. 20, Rue de l'Hirondelle, another entrance beckons you to linger. Behind you, the promise of delightful moments at Le Delhy's Hôtel. By all means, do set off to explore the romantic winding streets in this part of the quarter off Saint-Germain-des-Prés. It's a ballade (stroll) that will pluck the strings of your heart.

☺ *At the end of a long day, but this passage is closed from midnight to 6:00 AM*

🎎 *When the Paris night enfolds you in its arms*

♡ *The perfect setting!*

The Most Romantic Railway Station Platforms

Go ahead, steal a kiss on a railway station platform. Nobody is watching, and you won't feel out of place! Everybody is busy running to catch their train, or else kissing their dear ones goodbye. Railway station kisses in the whirl and crush of passengers can be wonderfully private!

Gare Montparnasse

Welcome to Gare Montparnasse! Arriving at platforms 11 to 15 are the drab, metallic gray suburban trains. These old suburban trains certainly have retro appeal especially if you're fond of the '60s and

'70s. All day long they discharge their freight of kissing lovers. The biggest crush of departing passengers is at evening rush hour. Arriving passengers leap into their awaiting lovers' outstretched arms before the screeching trains even come to a full stop. Isn't love beautiful?

🕐 *When school lets out or at evening rush hour*

🍫 *Go get a steaming cup of hot chocolate afterwards*

♥ *Feel the clickity-click of your racing heart as you embrace on a railway platform*

Gare de Lyon

More lovers have been enveloped in the swirling steam from the Paris-Venice night train than from any other train. And even if you aren't planning a departure tonight, you can still rendezvous on the platform and sigh as you take your beloved into your arms, both of you dreaming of that gondola ride under the Bridge of Sighs.

You should be aware that the platform numbers change every day: perfect for lovers who can't stand routine. And yet, punctuality is essential! Even if some have the annoying habit of making others wait, it's common knowledge that French trains always arrive and depart on time.

🕐 *Check with French Rail for a current timetable*

🕊 *Nostalgic!*

♥ *Leave the gondolas in Venice and come take my hand*

Bateaux-Mouches Smooches

8th arrondissement

Under Pont de l'Alma

Métro Alma-Marceau

Join the seagulls from the Normandy coast that glide on gale winds inland to seek refuge in Paris harbors. Meld into the anonymous crowd on the bateaux-mouches to sneak a smooch as the seagulls screech overhead. Shed that image of the most wanted lover west of the Pecos by immersing yourself in the throngs of tourist-passengers.

Purchase tickets for your dreamy river excursion under Pont de l'Alma. One last word of advice before departure: don't let the company photographer take your picture. Since photo-souvenirs are posted on a panel. You'll have a posse hot on your heels in no time!

🕐 *Weekends from 11:00 AM to 5:00 PM*

☼ *The more the merrier!*

♡ *Anchors away!*

Musée de la Vie Romantique

9th arrondissement

9, rue Chaptal – 01 48 74 95 38 – Open daily except on Mondays

Métro Blanche

On top of the hill in the Saint-Georges quarter, at the dawn of the Second Empire, a microcosm of poets, writers, actors and musicians gravitated toward the comfortable home of Ary Scheffer, illustrious painter of the Romantic era (1820–1850). The group included Chopin, whose finger dexterity was top notch, and George Sand. Every Friday evening, Delacroix, Ingres, Liszt, and Lamartine joined them. Today, the statue of Chopin at his piano takes us back to the atmosphere of those days. Soak up the 19th century ambiance at the Musée de la Vie Romantique (the museum of romanticism). Even the garden is romantic. Delightful scents of bellflowers, foxglove, clematis, and wild roses fill the courtyard. You'll feel transported back in time. Show your support for the tradition, and plan to rendezvous there every Friday.

🕐 *Between 10:00 AM and noon*

✿ *For the wild roses*

♡ *Okay, but keep it romantic!*

Boating in the Bois de Boulogne

16th arrondissement

RER station Avenue-Henri-Martin

While you, my good man, are decked out in a boatman's cap for the occasion, your pretty petty officer sports a darling white dress and twirls a lace parasol on her shoulder. Your uniforms are just right. No longer landlubbers! Mind you, some of these little boats are not entirely watertight. But what better excuse could you have to roll up your sleeves, take hold of your sweetheart's wet feet, and warm them with doting kisses. Then set course for the isle in the middle of the lake for a picnic on the grass. You'll have to do some serious rowing to be worthy of her kisses.

☺ *Set out early enough for a noontime picnic*

☼ *At least the boater's cap will be good for something*

♡ *Move back from the shore for discretion*

Under the Waterfall in the Bois de Boulogne

16th arrondissement

Bois de Boulogne

Métro La Muette or Ranelagh, or RER station Boulainvilliers

In the best adventure films, waterfalls always conceal magical entrances. But what lies behind the cascade in the Bois de Boulogne? Could it be the elephant cemetery of Paris? No, not at all. It's simply a hideaway for couples with a thirst for the exotic. Flee the hustle and bustle of city life and wander into this virgin forest where lovers embrace. A great place to play "Me Tarzan, You Jane." Swing on over to the Bois de Boulogne for new adventures.

☺ *After watching a great adventure film or a* Tarzan *rerun*

☼ *Loin cloths and bikinis!*

♡ *An aquatic curtain to steal behind*

Three Villas and a Hamlet

16th arrondissement

Métro Exelmans

What a great title for a summer TV miniseries this would make! Three villas and the Boileau hamlet, tucked away in the middle of the 16th arrondissement. In fact, it's actually the setting for a beautiful and great love story... yours! The first act takes place at the Villa Meyer, where you are kissing as the action begins. Here along flowered walkways, clustered together like a sweet bouquet, is a group of magnificent homes, each with its own little garden. The title of the second episode would be "Villa Cheysson." Splendid dwellings with ivy, hydrangeas, and cherry trees—the perfect setting for blossoming love. The third episode: Villa Dietz-Monin. Here you feel like you're on an island. The entrance to the villas is through Avenue Georges-Risler, located next to 25, rue Claude Lorrain. You steal the show at the climax of the film spending your golden years in the Boileau Hamlet—your own Paris remake of *On Golden Pond*. There you are, in the heart of this Paris village, sitting beside the La Fontaine traffic circle at the intersection of Impasse Racine and Avenue Molière, locked in an embrace, forever in love! The End.

🕐 *From 3:00 PM to 5:30 PM*

❀ *Spring flowers and abundant foliage*

♥ *Private property!*

Delicious... Bouches de Métro

The very term *"bouche de métro"* is an invitation for a kiss! Leave it to the French to call an entrance or opening a mouth (*bouche*)! At the appointed time of the rendezvous, you stand demurely in front of the metro waiting for lover-boy to appear. Anticipation grips you. Suddenly, you see that unmistakable smile. He bounds up the steps to wrap you in his arms. In his tender embrace you can't help but fix your eyes on the ornate wrought iron embracing the graceful orange lamps over the metro exit. Thank Mr. Guimard for designing Paris's most romantic metro exits!

Métro Abbesses

Patience, my dear! This metro station is the deepest underground station in Paris. It lies some 200 feet below the street level. It will take your sweetheart quite a while to reach the open air where you wait. Place des Abbesses is undoubtedly one of the most charming spots in all Paris. A nearby flower garden offers weary legs a well-deserved resting place. Doff the shoes and treat your honey to a delicious foot massage!

Metro Alexandre-Dumas
The tree-lined divider strip on Boulevard Charonne (at No. 115) is relatively calm for a major thoroughfare.

Métro Blanche
"I've been living for two months on Blanche Place. This winter has been one of the mildest on record. Women make brief but charming appearances at the café terrace, which seems to be a favorite for drug dealers," wrote André Breton, who gathered with his friends in the 1920s at "Le Cyrano" café, 82, boulevard de Clichy. Don't bother looking for it now as it has become a fast-food restaurant.

Métro Lamarck-Caulaincourt
The exit comes out directly below a Montmartre staircase. A flower shop seems to have sprung up there, just for you. Pick up a bouquet of forget-me-nots while you wait!

Métro Porte-Dauphine
Gentlemen, in anticipation of a delightful walk in the woods, rendezvous with your miss at Porte Dauphine. Improve your chances of getting what you want by greeting her at this sumptuous location. It's up to you to do the rest!

Métro Saint-Michel
The exit for Place Saint-André-des-Arts is superb. And you can stop for a drink right away at the café terrace of La Gentilhommière. Search no further! The wicker chairs, the kiosk, and the canopy of trees make this a stunning setting for romance.

Métro Saint-Paul
You don't mind pollution but you adore romantic places. This metro exit is for you! The exhaust from all those tail pipes in your face as you head up the steps won't prevent you from enjoying the charm of this little square.

3

Crazy Kisses

W hat would romance be without a touch of madness or a spark of imagination? Why not a fling on the roofs of Paris or a good chuckle in front of the distorting mirrors at the Jardin d'Acclimatation? For those willing to take a detour off the beaten path there is no end of unusual escapades, and a little craziness will sometimes make you brave enough to venture into forbidden territory. Everyone must weigh the pros and cons of encounters which, though innocent enough, may sometimes be illegal. Some of the craziest kissing experiences are the ones that really aggravate others, and you'll get a taste of those too at the end of this chapter.

On the Roofs

The moon is full. You stealthily set out on velvety paws making not a creak or a squeak on the polished parquet. Pry open the trapdoor in the ceiling and leap like two cats onto the mysterious Parisian rooftop of gray-blue zinc. Frolic in the moonlight at the edge of the gutters beneath the gleam of stars and street lamps. But don't try this adventure in the rain. And I would suggest, young fellow, that you avoid skipping from rooftop to rooftop to demonstrate the love your "feline" inspires in you. You've got plenty of other tricks in your little chimney sweep's kit.

� *Ask your cat! If he does not deign to answer, then follow him...
And if you don't have a cat, follow your neighbor's*

☼ *On hot, muggy nights*

♡ *One more thing: "When the monument lights go out, there are people who climb onto roofs and whoop it up. They kiss behind chimneys, and when it's warm out, they make love on the terraces,"
said Hippo to Nathalie in the Éric Rochant film* Love without Pity

Smooching in Tandem

3rd arrondissement
93, boulevard Beaumarchais
Métro Saint-Sébastien-Froissart

What is the ultimate in crazy kissing? Doing it on a bicycle... and with an anti-pollution mask on! Both sad and crazy, but with a zaniness that is much purer than the air we breathe! And yet kisses while cycling can also be rather funny, especially on a bike that's unusual or a collector's item. Not the kind you'd find at your run-of-the-mill sports store, but something from Cycl'Art, 93, boulevard Beaumarchais. If daring city cyclists like to lock onto cars while rolling along, then you can lock lips while riding in tandem! Nothing simpler! The front rider sits and pedals backwards, while the second rider calls the shots.

☺ *At dawn, or on days when metro workers are on strike (plenty of those in France!)*

⚜ *Pollution levels are lower in the wee-hours on winter mornings*

♡ *Be careful though because Parisian drivers are not particularly fond of cyclists*

Meet After Class!

4th arrondissement
14, rue Charlemagne
Métro Saint-Paul

Ah, school days! What could be more picturesque than a couple of teenagers kissing each other as they leave school? What do you think, Mr. Headmaster? Pretty recreational courts, covered play-grounds, and hallways... aren't they ideal locations? With your straight navy blue skirt and black shoes, mademoiselle, a ponytail, a little backpack, and a touch of lipstick... you're ready for your first kiss. Your heart beats wildly. Look, he's coming! He nonchalantly saunters out of Charlemagne High and waits for you beside the en-chanting fountain. Cool water, as everyone knows, is the natural complement of love.

☺ *After class*

⚜ *Rediscover the thrills of back to school*

♡ *Look out, here comes the principal!*

Aquatic Rendezvous at Place Saint-Michel

6th arrondissement
Saint-Michel Fountain
Métro Saint-Michel

What could be more typically Parisian than to make a date to meet at Place Saint-Michel? While it seems there is no place to sit except for the little concrete posts, if you look carefully you'll see there are seats provided. And what's more, they're always free. Nevertheless, even during bad weather, lovers prefer to wait for each other while standing in the rain rather than sitting in the spray from the fountain's two lion-shaped stone angels. Try it, it can be fun! But don't forget to protect your guidebook: it can still be very useful to you!

🕛 *Midnight. But no skinny-dipping!*
❄ *You wouldn't want to catch cold!*
♡ *Your reward for being so brave!*

Ride a Carrousel

7th, 12th, 16th, 18th and 20th arrondissements

Paris has plenty of pretty old-fashioned carrousels. Horsing around on a gaily-painted wood horse at dusk as the city lights start to twinkle can be soooo romantic, as can being serenaded by handled-bar-mustached gentlemen working grind organs. When the last few bars of a piped-in waltz die down, suavely kiss your cavalier or "cavalierette"! Young and old alike flock to these charming attractions throughout Paris: Place de la Nation, La Villette, Sacré-Cœur, the Eiffel Tower. Dizzyingly delightful.

🕛 *About 5:00 PM*
❄ *As the chilly of a winter evening sets in*
♥ *You'll be sharing the ride with children*

A Fine Place for an Enormous Bouquet

8th arrondissement
8, rue d'Anjou
Métro Madeleine

Marie Kalergis, a ravishing Russian aristocrat, resided at 8, rue d'Anjou. After boarding her daughter at the convent des Oiseaux, she plunged into Parisian social life in the company of her cousin, Lydia Nesselrode, and Princess Nadezhda Narischkina, her best friend. Money was no problem for her. Example: she once placed an order for flowers that came to 80,000 francs. This whopping sum was the equivalent of 44 years average income for a relatively well-paid worker (roughly 5 francs a day). Show up on the doorstep with your blossoming love affair.

☾ *Early evening*
⚌ *Because the streets are lacking flowers*
♡ *You've earned it, haven't you?*

A Peck and a Peek at the Presidential Palace

8th arrondissement
55, rue du Faubourg-Saint-Honoré
Métro Concorde

Beaujon, a wealthy 18th century financier slept in an enormous wickerwork basket hung like a hammock from four trees planted right in the middle of his bedroom. Outlandish ideas were certainly his cup of tea. He also liked to be rocked to sleep by seductive ladies… Today, his residence is none other than that of the President of the French Republic! Go ahead and give each other a little kiss in the courtyard of the Élysée Palace! An innocent peck would be nothing compared to some of the crazy things this place has seen.

☾ *Arrive early in the morning because there are so many amateurs*
⚌ *Doors are open for National Heritage Days, mid-September*
♡ *Who's going to stop you?*

The Splendid History of 25, Avenue des Champs-Élysées

8th arrondissement
Métro Franklin-D.-Roosevelt

Thérèse Lachmann, a modest young woman from Eastern Europe, took up residence in Paris, abandoning husband and child. Soon after her arrival, she reduced the pianist Hertz to poverty, then became ill. One day she fainted in front of the present No. 25, avenue des Champs-Élysées. She swore to herself that if she recovered she would become fabulously wealthy and build the most luxurious and impressive mansion in Paris on that very spot. So she did! The Marquis de Païva found her very attractive. Once they were married, he had this mansion built for her. Today, it is open to visitors. The bronze door was sculpted by Legrain. Paintings by Baudry and sculptures by Dalou grace the salons. An absolute must-see is the onyx staircase, which inspired this famous aphorism from Delacroix: "Vice, like virtue, has many steps." Megalomania reached incredible heights in this home. Nothing could rival the lavish receptions given by the Marquise de Païva.

The Marquise of Païva later became enamored of the Count Henckel von Donnersmarck, the young millionaire cousin of Bismarck. The Marquis committed suicide, and the Marquise became a countess. From demimonde to high society, there is but one step, providing you have the right shoes! Thérèse Lachmann would turn over in her grave if she knew that today No. 25 has become a currency exchange office! As for you, gentlemen, if you are the penny-pinching type, beware of fainting ladies at this address. Then again, some tender mouth-to-mouth resuscitation could do you some good...

☺ *Morning. Skip breakfast and feel faint*
☼ *A hot summer day, for the above reason*
♡ *Good excuse for mouth-to-mouth resuscitation*

Up in a Tree! It's Time to Branch Out!

9th arrondissement
Métro Trinité

What is the difference between a city tree and country tree? The urban specimen is absolutely off limits. Are city trees weaker than country trees? Are our shoes more damaging than exhaust fumes or smog? Not likely! Then why is it forbidden to climb them? Because that's the way it is! Which is a pity... because the *Pterocarya Fraxinifolia* is an invitation to all types of mischievous behavior. A 120-year-old tree in front of the stunning Church of the Trinity

seems to be praying, with its enormous branches raised heaven-
ward, that some day two lovers will come and bill and coo in the
crook of its arms.

☺ *Early morning*

✿ *Hide in the spring foliage*

♥ *Up higher! Here comes the caretaker!*

A Kiss at Full Gallop

12th arrondissement

Bois de Vincennes

Métro Château-de-Vincennes or Bus 112 at the Cartoucherie stop

How about doubling up on a saddle with your Amazon for some
horsing around in the Bois de Vincennes? Don't bridle at the idea:
ride with your bride! Gently place a soft kiss upon her neck. With
the stallion's cadenced pace, let your passions gallop away—and
onwards to the royal castle! You may have to lift her long, beautiful
mane to bury your lips burning with desire. The dream of every
young maiden is to be swept away by a prince on a white steed! So
saddle up at the equestrian center of La Cartoucherie. However, if
you're shy of horses, perhaps you should head over to the Pony Club
at the Post House on Route de Suresnes in the Bois de Boulogne.

☺ *9:30 AM–11:00 AM*

❄ *A blanket of snow on the ground, just like in fairy tales*

♡ *Only on the neck*

A Shower of Smooches at Parc André-Citroën

15th arrondissement

33, rue de la Montagne-de-l'Espérou

Métro Javel

Even if you are not officially allowed to shower under the spray of
the fountains at the André-Citroën Park, breaking rules makes some
people's mouths water. Go ahead and enjoy the spray! Get soaking
wet! Belt out a few hit songs—with or without an umbrella.
Supertramp's *It's Raining Again* or Gene Kelly's *I'm Singing in the
Rain* will do just fine. Who can resist the temptation? Unlike all
other Parisian fountains, this one has no basin. The water gushes

out of a slab in the ground. You've got it! You can do your own Barefoot in the Park! Afterwards, dry those feet off in one of the two greenhouses beside the fountain. Fragrant eucalyptus trees smell so good! Two little wooden benches beneath the greenhouse glass seem to be cultivating a torrid love. Try the bench under the palm trees. The more exotic the better!

🕒 *The forbidden shower is open Monday to Friday: 7:30 AM–7:30 PM, weekends and holidays: 9:00 AM–7:30 PM*

☼ *When green flags fly on the beaches in France*

♡ *As a finish to* I'm Singing in the Rain

Deformed Kisses

16th arrondissement
Jardin d'Acclimatation
Bois de Boulogne
Métro Les Sablons

Crack up laughing in front of the distorting mirrors at the Jardin d'Acclimatation. One moment you're Laurel, and the next you're Hardy. Your lips will look thin or full, fleshy, shriveled, or puffed up like French pastry. It all depends on which mirror you choose.

🕒 *10:00 AM–6:30 PM*

⚘ *Bare those arms and legs*

♡ *Even distorted by the mirrors, your lover is still the fairest of them all!*

Like Louis XIII, Everybody in the Seine!

16th arrondissement
Métro Passy

Chilly water hardly bothered adventurous King Louis XIII. He and his son enjoyed frequent swims in the River Seine near the Passy quarter. In fact, during the 17th century, dips in the Seine were quite the fashion. Some Parisians tossed all modesty to the wind, and wearing nothing but their birthday suits they would plunge into the Seine in the very center of Paris! They took quite a chance because back then, nudists were punished by beatings and were paraded through the streets of Paris in their nightshirts.

Former mayor of Paris Jacques Chirac, and former Environment Minister Ségolène Royal ought to be held to their word. Both promised that once pollution in the river was cleaned up, they would swim in the Seine. Right now, it would be foolhardy to dive in and even more so to kiss underwater. You might try with your mouths closed, but, then again, why bother? Perhaps someone's mouth should have stayed shut before making promises that evaporate like water!

☾ *The water is always chilly*

☼ *Summer for your best bet*

♡ *Sirens may be lurking*

Caricature of a Kiss

18th arrondissement

Place du Tertre

Métro Abbesses or Anvers, then funicular or stairs

Head up to Place du Tertre and immortalize your most artistic kiss! All year round on this pretty square, you will find caricature artists more than happy to lengthen your nose, puff up your lips, give you bulging eyes, or make your freckles pretty perky. Posing can be pleasant indeed as it allows you time to enjoy a smooch—and the longer the better! Why display a humdrum photo of your wedding kiss on the fireplace mantle back home, when you can impress family and friends with your sulfurous portraits as heroes on the cover of a dime novel?

☾ *Sundown for that romantic afterglow effect*

⛄ *When Montmartre sends its tourists off to the ski slopes*

♡ *Hold that pose and don't move!*

The "I Love You" Wall

18th arrondissement

Square des Abbesses, Place des Abbesses

Métro Abbesses

With Saint Valentine's Day, lovers have long had their own special day on the calendar. But did you know that they also have their own special wall? And best of all, that wall is located in the ultra-romantic Montmartre quarter of Paris. Gazillions of "I-love-you" messages are penciled, stenciled, painted, and carved into this wall. The point of departure for the creator of the wall, Frédéric Baron, was a *Round the World in 80...* Ways—that is: 80 ways to say "I love you." Phileas Fogg would be proud! Mr. Baron asked his brother to write the magic phrase in French—*Je t'aime!* Then he asked his neighbors to contribute in Arabic, Portuguese, Russian, and every other language spoken in this multiethnic quarter of Paris. Not one to leave good-enough alone, he visited embassies and collected over three hundred versions of the phrase. Globally, I'd say it's delightful! Repeat after me: *Assavakkit! Munsmawa! Te iubesc! Ndakuyanda! Rojai ju!* No, these are not tongue twisters... they are heart warmers!

🕐 *8 AM to avoid the tourists. But check for time zone changes!*
❀ *Although there's really no season for saying "I love you"*
♡ *This little square is nicely tucked away*

Trying on a Wedding Gown

18th arrondissement
Tati – 5, rue Belhomme
Métro Barbès-Rochechouart

There's no obligation to actually buy or become engaged to your favorite "mannequin." But you can let your imaginations run wild as you don the appropriate attire. Oh how delicious your wedding kiss would be! The ceremony takes place in the fitting rooms at Tati or in one of these specialty stores: Pronuptia, 66, boulevard Raspail (6th arrondissement), Rêve d'un Jour, 33, rue d'Amsterdam (9th arrondissement), or Ronald Joyce, 5, rue d'Hauteville (10th arrondissement).

🕐 *In the waning hours of your bachelorhood*
❀ *When else, my dears?*
♡ *Don't forget to draw the changing booth curtain*

Slip and Slide

20th arrondissement
84, rue des Couronnes
Métro Couronnes

The trip to the crest of Belleville Hill for the toboggan run begins at the stairway facing number 84, rue des Couronnes. Hand in hand, scale the mount straight to the top. Just before you reach it, a rock on the right (excuse me, the "concrete blob," because this is modern Belleville) offers a cozy love nest. On to the left, three toboggans are set up at the entrance to Parc de Belleville. No turning back now! You're at the top of the slide. Sit face to face and hold your sweetheart tight, as the braver of the two of you will be going down the slide backwards. Let go and whoosh! Enjoy it while you can. It's all over so fast.

If you have children, tell them to go play ball with the little champs on the fields. The ambiance and intimacy here is perfect. There are other toboggans at Parc de la Villette and Aquaboulevard if you're not completely thrilled.

☺ *From 8:30 AM–7:00 PM. Avoid weekends and Wednesdays since you will feel you have to let the little ones go first*
🐸 *Mud puddles galore!*
♥ *Little monsters can pop up at any moment*

Waltzing Matilda at City Hall

20th arrondissement
6, place Gambetta
Métro Gambetta

No other Paris district city hall inspires a little fooling around like the 20th arrondissement city hall. During the Second Empire, "L'Île d'Amour," a rip-roaring Belleville dance hall, had hearts waltzing all over the place. Today the old dance hall has been replaced by this government building where the district mayor unites couples in matrimony. What dress should you wear? A party dress or a wedding gown? Try both!

☺ *Noon for the wedding dress and 10:00 PM for the evening gown*
🐸 *From May 15 to July 15*
♡ *Say, "I do!"*

Aggravating Kisses

Brigade des mineurs

1st arrondissement
Police headquarters
12, quai de Gesvres
Métro Châtelet

Madame or Mademoiselle, you look younger than your age, almost like a teenager or a mere child. Put on a plaid skirt, white socks, tie your hair in pigtails. Monsieur, gray your hair and mustache, or put on a fake beard and an oversized beige trench coat and enjoy a fun new game with your partner. Loiter a while in front of the juvenile protection office (*Brigade de Protection des Mineurs*), waiting for her to skip innocently by. Open your trench coat and hoarsely call out to her, "What some candy, little girl?" Dangerous, but fun if you have nothing better to do.

☉ *1:00 PM when the bureaucrats file out to grab lunch*
✿ *So you'll look very out of place in that trench coat*
♡ *You might have to take it on the lam!*

Mona Lisa Won't Mind

1st arrondissement
Louvre Museum – Open daily except on Tuesdays
Métro Palais-Royal–Musée-du-Louvre

For you who dream of being as famous as *The Mona Lisa*, here is your chance for photographic fame. All you have to do is stand between the painting and the tourists wildly snapping their cameras at her. Get ready to be yelled at. Then again, some amateur filmmaker might particularly appreciate having the footage of your kiss for a slow motion sequence in a homemade production! You never know!

☉ *2:00–5:00 PM*
✿ *July, in the height of tourist season*
♡ *The longest-lasting gags are always the best*

Kissing on the Moving Sidewalk

6th and 15th arrondissements
Gare Montparnasse
Métro Montparnasse-Bienvenüe

In the seemingly endless corridors of the Montparnasse-Bienvenüe metro and train station, have some fun with the longest languorous French kissing possible on the rolling sidewalk. You will seriously annoy passengers scurrying and racing to catch their trains. This trick never fails! It's splendid riding along and feeling the little bumping under your feet!

🕒 *7:00 PM, during evening rush hour*

🎀 *Spring it on them!*

♡ *Distance is on your side (1600 feet)!*

National Assembly

7th arrondissement
33, quai d'Orsay
Métro Assemblée-Nationale or Invalides

A few seats are reserved for the general public to observe legislators at work in the National Assembly. While lawmakers strive for eloquence, you show off your knowledge of French history by engaging in a *baiser de Lamourette* (see definition on page 105). Shoot for a Wednesday when legislative sessions are broadcast live on television. Chances are that the cameramen will be bored, and you may get a starring role!

🕒 *1:00 PM–9:30 PM on Tuesdays. 3:00 PM–9:30 PM Wednesdays and Thursdays (sometimes 9:00 AM 1:00 PM). Show up early because only the first 10 get seats*

🎀 *In October, when delegates return to session*

♡ *Ham it up for your first screen role!*

Both in a Booth

Anywhere in the city

Locate a single telephone booth, not several grouped together. Wait until it starts to rain cats and dogs, and you feel an irrepressible sudden urge for kissing! Before you get totally soaked, take shelter in the telephone booth. Stay there as long as you like and gloat while others hurl their insults at you. The line grows longer and the grumbling grows louder. "Plenty of other places where they can do that! Really! Some of us need to place a phone call!" "Hey in there! You're only allowed up to six minutes!" "I'm going to drag you out of there m'self! You wait and see!" Some friendly advice: exit the booth before you're pulled out.

☺ *Between noon and 2:00 PM*

🦋 *On a rainy autumn days so that aggression reaches a climax more quickly*

♡ *Long kisses aggravate bystanders but they are oh, so exciting!*

Upstaging the Actors

Any movie theater in Paris

People absorbed in watching a film pay little attention to lovers in dark movie theaters. When a bigger-than-life kiss in Technicolor fills the screen, copy that passionate embrace for all to see. Leap out of your seats and plant yourselves up there in front of the screen while the audience applauds, cheers, hoots, and jeers. It doesn't even have to be a showing of the cult *Rocky Horror Picture Show*.

☺ *Saturday showings from 8:00 PM to midnight*

🦋 *Go on a rainy night. You've got better venues for kissing when the weather is nice*

♡ *Like movie stars*

At a Green Light

In posted no-stopping zones

You're behind the steering wheel of your car. Suddenly behind you a taxi driver or bus driver or someone driving a BMW or cherry red convertible with suburban plates really ticks you off by honking their horn before the light even turns green. Teach them a lesson! Wait it out for the next light and enjoy (along with your passenger) a long smooch. Lap up the seething impatience of the harried drivers stuck behind your vehicle. One detail: experience has taught us to remember to set the hand brake. A few spots that we have tested for you: the busy Champs-Elysées, Boulevard Sébastopol, and Boulevard Magenta, and the always congested Rue de Rivoli.

🕐 *5:30 PM–7:30 PM*

🚦 *The traffic department will give you the green light*

♡ *Keep an eye on the rearview mirror all the same!*

4

Celluloid Kisses

I n the 1940s, Japan censored kisses on the silver screen. Ditto for India, but the task of censorship was relegated to the projectionist. At each torrid scene, the projection lamp had to be turned off. Imagine screening Don Juan, an American film from 1926 that included no fewer than 127 kisses! Since the earliest reels, American cinema has featured countless kissing scenes, and holds the record for the longest cinematic kiss: 3 minutes and 5 seconds. Thank you, Jane Wyman (the future Mrs. Ronald Reagan), and Regis Toomey. French cinema has titillated us with fewer torrid scenes, but made Paris the backdrop for many great love stories with certain unforgettable embraces.

Les Amants du Pont-Neuf (The Lovers on the Bridge, 1999)

1st arrondissement
Pont-Neuf
Métro Pont-Neuf

Let's set the record straight: *Les Amants du Pont-Neuf* was filmed in great part in Lansargues, outside Montpellier, on a reconstructed set. When Léos Carax made this film, he wanted to free himself from production constraints of filming in Paris. But your lover will be all the more thrilled if you insist that the Pont-Neuf in Paris was the actual location where Denis Lavant and Juliette Binoche danced their diabolic waltz as July 14 fireworks shot off and lit up the night sky.

🕛 *Midnight*
☼ *July 14*
♡ *Beneath the statue of Henri IV*

Diva (1981)

1st arrondissement
Théâtre du Châtelet – 1, place du Châtelet
Métro Châtelet

After a performance at the Théâtre du Châtelet, go up on stage once the audience has left. Wait for your diva to come and take you by the hand. Then the two of you can share the final kiss of the Jean-Jacques Beineix film, with the soundtrack blasting in the headphones of your Walkman. If you haven't internalized the character of a postal worker yet, try stealing a mailman's uniform and a revealing outfit for your darling soprano who has been warming up her vocal cords in the shower. On the appointed day, breathe deeply to control your stage fright. Then let your musical explosion of joy shatter glass!

🕐 *After the performance*
🧣 *Scarves or boas for that sore throat*
♡ *Rehearse during the performance!*

Violette et François (1977)

1st arrondissement
Gardens of the Palais-Royal
Métro Palais-Royal

Early in the morning, beneath the arcades at the Palais-Royal gardens, François (played by Jacques Dutronc) drives up on his Solex. Violette (Isabelle Adjani) runs towards him and throws herself in his arms. François lets go of his motorized bicycle and kisses Violette royally. In this 1970s film by Jacques Rouffio, Isabelle Adjani and Jacques Dutronc portray an explosive couple. François's occupation is shoplifting in major department stores, and he tries to teach Violette the ropes. Play it safe. Stick to replaying the kissing scene—you don't want to wind up arrested. In terms of accessories, a scooter will do the trick. It's a lot easier to find than an old black Solex. Charming they were, but running Solexes are mighty hard to find nowadays.

🕐 *Early in the morning*
🧣 *In the fog*
♡ *Make these two great actors proud of you*

Lunes de fiel (Bitter moon, 1992)

4th arrondissement
Square Jean-XXIII, next to Notre-Dame Cathedral
Métro Cité, RER station Saint-Michel–Notre-Dame

A sleepless night has passed. Early morning fog creeps over Square Jean-XXIII. Sitting on a bench next to Emmanuelle Seigner, Peter Coyote massages her feet and lovingly breathes on them to warm them. What woman would refuse to change places with the actress here? Waste not a minute! Select a bench between Notre-Dame and the Seine. The dense concentration of lovers on the benches facing away from the cathedral makes this a far-too-popular lovers' lane. Thanks to Roman Polanski, director of *Lunes de Fiel*, for urging all us Quasimodos to take better care of our Esmeraldas' feet... and vice versa. Another game for lovers on the square: tossing bread crumbs in the air for the sparrows accustomed to the crowds around Notre-Dame. Watch them catch the crumbs in mid-flight while wide-eyed children stare.

☺ *Sunrise*
🎿 *Frosty toes to massage*
♡ *Frosty toes to gently kiss*

Charade (1963)

5th arrondissement
Quai de Montebello and boat cruise
RER station Saint-Michel–Notre-Dame

In 1963, *Charade* brought Cary Grant and Audrey Hepburn together on the screen for the first time. In this American film by Stanley Donen, Audrey Hepburn plays a woman who finds out that her husband has been murdered. Four of his old Army buddies pursue the beautiful Audrey. They are convinced that she knows where her husband hid his stolen gold bullion. Cary Grant follows her to Paris and offers to help her out. But she doesn't know if she can trust him. After a memorable scene in which Cary Grant takes a shower while completely dressed, the couple meets for dinner on a pleasure boat. While standing on the deck of the boat, they see a couple on a bench at the far end of the Quai de Bourbon locked in an amorous embrace. Then, they notice another couple leaning against a tree. Our heroine murmurs in Carry's ear, "You don't look so bad in this light." He galantly replies: "Why do you think I brought you here." A few minutes later, through the magic of cinema, they exchange a ten-second Hollywood-style kiss! This scene, like the rest of the film, was shot on location. Don't give it a second thought: buy a ticket for the love boat now!

🌃 *Exterior, night*

🌸 *Sizzling*

♡ *Happy ending guaranteed*

Un monde sans pitié (Love without Pity, 1989)

6th arrondissement
Luxembourg Gardens
RER station Luxembourg

No pity for Hippo! In this 1989 Eric Rochant film, Hippo (played by Hippolyte Girardot) is smitten by Nathalie (Mireille Perrier). But to Hippo's immense regret, Nathalie—a brilliant graduate of the École Normale Supérieure and a translator of Russian—is a workaholic. But in spite of that, they find time to rendezvous... and kiss in Luxembourg Gardens. A classic kiss in fin-de-siècle cinema.

Want to follow their example? Wonder where you should go to steal a kiss? Easy! Luxembourg Gardens, of course, with the Pantheon as a backdrop. But be forewarned! The tender encounter between our two lovebirds is short-lived. Nathalie has to leave for work. Hippo thunders, "Thirty thousand chicks here and the only one who's splitting is the one I am interested in." He yells at some girls in the garden, "Get the hell out of here! Go on, everybody, go back to work! Go see your... Russians, but let me have her!" Nothing can convince Nathalie to stay. Let's hope, though, that you will be luckier than poor, pitiful Hippo!

🌃 *Mid-afternoon*

🌸 *A beautiful autumn day*

♡ *As torrid as any early romance*

French Kiss (also titled Paris Match, 1995)

8th arrondissement
Hôtel George V
31, avenue George-V
Métro George-V

In *French Kiss*, a comedy by Lawrence Kasdan, Meg Ryan (the effervescent blonde in *When Harry Met Sally*) flies to Paris to confront her straying fiancé. Who does she see as she sweeps into the hotel to check in? There in the magnificent lobby of the Hotel George V, is her fiancé, locked in a languorous embrace (love, American style!) with a perfect stranger, a stunningly beautiful French chick! Our shocked heroine passes out. Now that you know the basics of the scene, and the setting, it's up to you to prove your acting abilities. Just one thing, though, not just anybody can slip into this prestigious hotel.

☺ *Improvisations can take place any time*
🦋 *Before Halloween*
♥ *Don't make anybody pass out*

Subway (1985)

9th arrondissement
RER station Auber

In the vast underground corridor of this subway station, at the bottom of the center staircase, Héléna (Isabelle Adjani) kisses Fred (Christophe Lambert) as a reply to his question "Don't you love me just a little?" Oh, femme fatale! Avoid this film's fatal ending—director Luc Besson kills off the hero in the end. Write your own scenario without the tragic ending. Plan your rendezvous in the central connecting hall at the RER station Auber. Then you can pucker up too, in response to the inevitable question "Don't you love me just a little?"

☺ *Rush hour*
☼ ❄ *Great shelter from the heat or cold*
♥ *Standing up, people are watching you*

Funny Face (1957)

10th arrondissement
Gare du Nord
Métro Gare-du-Nord

In this enchanting 1957 musical comedy by Stanley Donen, the great Fred Astaire plays fashion photographer Dick Avery. Standing on the arrivals platform for the London-Paris train, he photographs his model (Audrey Hepburn), who represents the typical American woman in Paris. He gives her a few pointers. "Now listen closely: today you're not happy. Right, now you're a creature of tragedy: heartbroken, suffering; you're Anna Karenina." "Shall I throw myself under the train?" she asks innocently. "We'll see," he answers, then mischievously adds, "But for now, just wonderful, noble self-sacrifice. Now, your lover has just kissed you goodbye. You may never know that kiss again; you may never know love again!" Having craftily planned his move, he tenderly gives her a demonstration. Surprised at first, Audrey Hepburn quickly appears enchanted. Good going, Fred! Ever so elegant! Now it's your turn to play out the scene.

☺ *Pick up the train schedule*
✿ *In a summer outfit*
♡ *You, too, should be original*

Chacun cherche son chat
(When the Cat's Away, 1996)

11th arrondissement
Pause Café Bastille
41, rue de Charonne
Métro Ledru-Rollin

There you stand in front of the Pause Café, a Bastille neighborhood bar. You give a pretty girl your telephone number, and before you walk away, you kiss her on the neck. Purrrrfect! This is exactly what happens between Benoît and his ravishing neighbor Chloé, who has just helped him move. In *Chacun cherche son chat*, by Cédric Klapisch, the magic kiss gives wings to pretty Chloé who scampers full speed down the sidewalk on Rue de Charonne. The regulars in the bar sing in unison, "*Paris, c'est une blonde...*"

(Paris is a blonde.) Right on the money, because even Paris is a character in this unusual film.

☺ *Cocktail hour*

🎔 *Watch Missy run down the sidewalks in a pretty spring frock!*

♡ *Regale the regulars with what's already regular at this café*

J'embrasse pas (I Don't Kiss, 1991)

16th arrondissement
Chalet des Îles – Bois de Boulogne
Métro La Muette or RER station Avenue-Henri-Martin

As the title indicates, there are no kissing scenes in the film *I Don't Kiss* by André Téchiné. But there is a particularly romantic breakfast-scene with Emmanuelle Béart and Manuel Blanc both playing prostitutes. After spending the night at the police station, the couple ends up at the Chalet des Îles restaurant in the Bois de Boulogne, which as the name indicates is on an island in the middle of the lake. They are alone in a sumptuous hall. Emmanuelle Béart, who has her heart set on becoming a singer, gives her rendition of *Sophie de Nantes*. As they leave the restaurant on the little motor-boat connecting the island with the shore, Emmanuelle Béart gently asks: "Would you like to sleep with me?" Use your imagination to come up with an ending for your love story. Don't expect the interior decoration in the restaurant to be identical; things have since changed. But the name of the dining room still is "La Pergola", and the charm of the place is perfectly intact.

☺ *For breakfast (as you leave the police station, if you can)*

🎔 *No crowds*

♡ *They don't, but you do!*

La Belle Verte (1996)

16th arrondissement
Parc des Princes Stadium
Métro Porte-de-Saint-Cloud

Plop onto the cushy green at the Parc des Princes. Run, dance, frolic, kick up a storm like the boisterous soccer players in this film by Coline Serreau. The well-written scenario features three characters from outer space who use their telepathic powers to discombobulate the players and a referee as well. Sitting up in the bleachers watching and redirecting the action, they send the players into a frenzied choreography that ends with a sulfurous and rather "gay" hug between two of the players. Now you know, and now the ball's in your field! Come on, let's play ball, boys!

☾ *At half-time*

✿ ✿ ✿ ✿ *No time out for lovers!*

♡ *Expect applause if the stands are jam-packed with fans!*

Ultimo Tango a Parigi (Last Tango in Paris, 1972)

16th arrondissement

Métro Bir-Hakeim

At the heart of this film by Bernardo Bertolucci is an "amusing" fight scene that pits Maria Schneider against her husband, Jean-Pierre Léaud. Since the film was first shown in 1972, it has sparked a lively critical debate due to its sexual violence. At one point, the couple is having a fist fight on the Bir-Hakeim station platform, finally falling into each others' arms and making up. The two protagonists kiss sitting on the ground in front of an advertisement. Try doing the same and observe the reaction of passersby.

☾ *Rush hour*

✿ *Warm things up!*

♡ *After the scuffle*

La Bête humaine (The Human Beast, 1938)

17th arrondissement

Square des Batignolles and SNCF depot Cardinet

Métro Brochant

"Let go of my hands! And don't look at me like that! You'll wear out your eyes," the boss's wife spat at railroad man Jacques Lantier (Jean Gabin). And, no, he doesn't reply with a "You've got gorgeous eyes, ya' know," because this wasn't Michele Morgan on the *Quai des Brumes*. The action takes place on a bridge near the Square des Batignolles. They don't embrace here, but across the way at the SCNF depot (Cardinet station). Totally smitten with the woman, Jean Gabin has her get on the train. He only gets a little peck on the cheek at this point. But, later in the evening, in the same depot, they have a more physical encounter. "Were you waiting for me?" asks the handsome railroad man. "Yes, I was waiting for you. I love you, Jacques," she says... just like in the movies. Jacques replies: "No kidding! You love me! Well then, I guess I have to tell you..." But he hardly has the time to tell her anything before she is kissing him passionately. Those of you who are fond of spine-tingling encounters may enjoy similar exciting moments in dark railway depots. But be careful! A beast lurks within you... Before you go any further, remember that poor Jacques Lantier went crazy with love, killed his beauty, then threw himself out of the train.

☺ *Middle of the day in the garden. Night at the train depot*

🏵 *Batignolles Square is splendid in spring!*

♡ *Of course you're not with Jean Gabin, but your guy's a sight for sore eyes, too!*

Les Quatre Cents Coups (The 400 Blows, 1959)

17th arrondissement

Place de Clichy

Métro Place-de-Clichy

Where is the best spot for an adulterous kiss? By the railing at the metro Place de Clichy, on the dividing strip! Keep your eyes open: kissing in the bushes may be fun, but a naughty little kid skipping class might catch you in the act. Recreate the famous scene from François Truffaut's *Quatre Cents Coups*, which won him an award at the Cannes film festival. Quiet on the set! Action!

☺ *Any time's a fine time to skip class*

👗 *In a vintage 1959 fur coat*

♥ *Watch out for a surprise visitor*

Le Fabuleux Destin d'Amélie Poulain
(Amélie from Montmartre, 2001)

18th arrondissement
Montmartre - Sacré-Cœur
Métro Anvers or Abbesses

No first kiss unless lover-boy has worked hard for it! The wiliest and most romantic types will set up a veritable obstacle course. For your first date, follow sweet Amélie's example and lead your beau (or belle) on a wild-goose chase. You'll need a piece of blue chalk. Draw arrows on the steep steps to point the way to the Sacré-Cœur basilica and entice your beau (or belle) to follow those marks. They'll take him (or her) right up to the panoramic telescope in front of the church. Position the viewfinder so that your beloved will see you and you alone, standing beside the carrousel far below. As your sweetheart rushes back down those steps towards you, dodge and hide. Relish the pleasure of teasing him (or her) with yet another rendezvous. Then again, you may decide to reward him (or her) with a kiss right then and there. But if you're like Amélie, you'll make him (or her) stew a good while longer. Anticipation never tasted so good!

☺ *Mid afternoon*
✿ *When flowery summer skirts bloom in the gardens of Sacré-Cœur*
♥ *You sweetie will be all out of breath and will need tender loving care*

Le Dernier Métro
(The Last Metro, 1980)

18th arrondissement
Théâtre de l'Atelier
1, place Charles-Dullin
Métro Anvers

Even though the film was shot in studio, the legendary theater house that inspired François Truffaut is worth a detour. Sneak into a dressing room, and close the door. Bernard—you can call yourself that even if you're not exactly built like Gérard Depardieu—you're going to plant one on your heroine as she leans against the wall. Imagine that you're face-to-face with Catherine Deneuve. When she tells you: "Goodbye, Bernard," give her a big juicy one, Depardieu-style. If things go according to the movie, your partner will confess, "I thought you were involved with every woman except me." So, without stammering, you shoot back, "First of all, not every woman; and, secondly, you intimidate me. Sometimes your expression was so unfeeling, even cruel." Oh, Bernard, Bernard, Bernard! How wrong you were about her! Can't you see how she really feels about you? She found your manly charms disturbingly attractive. Desire flames within the two of you! Hey, now, control yourselves. No rolling about on the floor. We seriously recommend you take the action back to your place!

🕐 *The last metro is at 12:45 AM*

⚖ *Wrap it up!*

♥ *Everything will be fine provided your spouse is not hiding in the cellar*

Casque d'Or (Golden Marie, 1952)

20th arrondissement
Rue Piat, Rue du Transvaal
Métro Belleville

Is she blonde? Ravishing? Cheeky? Are you crazy 'bout that dame? Step back in time to 1952. Belleville. Jacques Becker, director of the masterpiece *Casque d'Or*, leads you on the trail to a passionate kiss between Simone Signoret (playing a streetwalker) and Serge Reggiani (as Manda). Casque d'or alights from her carriage on Rue Piat. Brace yourselves for a jolt, gents. To faithfully reenact the scene, this kiss must be followed by a walloping slap, administered by your own Casque d'or. You see, Manda had somehow "forgotten" to tell her that he was already engaged.

The new Parc de Belleville has since brought some major changes to the landscape, but time travelers will find the hilltop area still recognizable. Today, the area where the scene was shot is no longer a wasteland. The place to deposit your kiss is right in front of 13, rue du Transvaal.

🕐 *Breakfast time*

🏵 *Enjoy the park*

♡ *Brace yourself for the slap!*

Les Enfants du paradis
(Children of Paradise, 1945)

20th arrondissement
Ménilmontant quarter
Métro Ménilmontant

In the *Children of Paradise*, a great classic of French cinema, the celebrated mime Debureau (Jean-Louis Barrault) burns with love for a small-time actress named Garance (Arletty). A scene takes place one evening on Ménilmontant hill. Jacques Prévert, the screenwriter for the film by Marcel Carné, penned the celebrated dialogues that rolled off the actors' lips: "What an odd fellow you are," Garance says with longing in her voice. Frédéric: "How beautiful you are... and the light in your eyes..." Garance: "Oh, the light, a little gleam, just like anybody. Look at all the little lights of Ménilmontant. People go to sleep and wake up. They all have lights that flicker on then off. Goodness, you're trembling! Are you cold?" she asks, worried. "I am trembling because I am happy. I am happy because you're here, near me. I love you. Garance, do you love me?" She places her arms on Frédéric's shoulders and declares: "You are the sweetest man I ever met!" Then after a touching "I love you," they kiss each other passionately. Garance draws back from Frédéric's lips and whispers the famous line: *"C'est tellement simple l'amour!"* ("Love's so simple!") At that precise moment, a dramatic clap of thunder rocks Ménilmontant. The two actors didn't play their scene on the actual streets of Ménilmontant, but in the Francoeur Studio (18th arrondissement). Nevertheless, you can make your cinematic pilgrimage to "Ménilmuche" as Parisians affectionately call the area.

🕒 *At night*
🏃 *For real shivers*
♡ *Love is so simple*

L'Année Juliette (1995)

Orly International Airport
RER station Orly

What is the best way to dissuade your mistress from moving in with you? Tough, especially for someone who simply can't say no. Need a suggestion? Lie! In *L'Année Juliette* by Philippe Le Guay, Camille, played by Fabrice Luchini, seems to have found the trick. He makes up a story about also being involved with a flutist who is away most of the time playing concerts. The perfect lie, perhaps. But perfect lies have a nasty habit of turning against you. They can really leave you smarting, especially when a big jealous lug sees his sweetheart in the arms of another man and lets his best uppercut fly. Golly, it was all just a ploy hatched by Camille himself to scare his pesky mistress off. For those of you who like flirting with danger, the scene takes place at Orly Airport. All you have to do is walk up to a pretty stranger picked out of the crowd, whisper in her ear, "Help me please, Miss! See that woman behind me? We're supposed to fly off to Italy today. But she wants us to have a baby. Just say that you are Juliette. Your name's Juliette Graveur, and your a flutist, a musician…" If everything goes according to the screenplay, she will reply, "Wouldn't it be more effective if I kissed you in front of her?" Here's where it all becomes a bit more dangerous. You have to go through with it, even if it means getting your jaw busted.

☺ *Just before boarding for a romantic trip to Italy*

✿ *Things could get pretty hot!*

♡ *Make it worth the trip out to Orly*

Masculin féminin (1966), or Masculine masculine!

Anywhere in Paris

Two gay men engage in a torrid kiss in the toilet of a typically Parisian brasserie when a young man disturbs their intimate moment by opening the door. "Get lost, twit" one of them barks. The hurt kid scrawls an angry message on the door, and leaves it at that. Through the romantic tribulations of a somewhat confused young man (Jean-Pierre Léaud), Jean-Luc Godard describes what café life was like in 1966 for a generation caught between antiwar demonstrations and the Beatles. The film deals with major issues of the day, such as the Vietnam War, the Pill... and free love. We won't be able to provide the address of the brasserie in the film: the owners don't want to repaint the toilet doorway every time you go through! However, for your own "New Wave" kiss, you will find a number of typically Parisian brasseries in each of the capital's arrondissements. One characteristic feature: toilets are most usually located in the basement.

⏱ *This time the romantic clock has the right to remain silent*
🍂 *When it's raining and there is nothing to do outside*
♡ *Good news!*

The Most Romantic Movie Theaters

Le Grand Rex
2nd arrondissement
1, boulevard Poissonnière
Métro Bonne-Nouvelle

The adjective "grand" is not grandiose enough to describe this superb Parisian movie theater that will take you through magical realms. The stars will not only twinkle in your lover's adoring eyes, but up on the ceiling, too. Thanks to a crescent beam of light glancing off particles of glass, a magical constellation awaits you in the hush of this temple of cinema. In 1957, Mylène Demongeot and Gary Cooper came to inaugurate the world's first escalator built for a movie theater. At the Grand Rex, you always see life and cinema on a grand scale. So bring the great love of your life, or even your sweetheart of the day.

⏱ *11:00 AM, tranquillity guaranteed*
🎋 *Exotic ambiance guaranteed*
♡ *Uncensored version guaranteed*

Double Armchairs at Europa Panthéon

5th arrondissement
13, rue Victor-Cousin
Métro Cluny-La-Sorbonne, RER station Luxembourg

Don't like to be separated by the armrest in movie theater seats? This is the place to come! Inseparable lovers will be pleasantly surprised to find four two-seaters! They're at the far end of the balcony at the Europa Panthéon. They really know how to spoil you there!

🕐 *1:30 PM*
🍂 *Chilly drizzly days*
♡ *Unless the film is a real thriller*

La Pagode

7th arrondissement
57 bis, rue de Babylone
Métro Saint-François-Xavier

La Pagode was the result of a magnificent love story at the end of the last century. Monsieur Morin, founder of the Bon Marché department store, was deeply in love with his wife. She couldn't resist any imported Chinese or Japanese goods. The Oriental style was quite fashionable in their day. Ever ready to please her, Monsieur Morin commissioned his architect, Alexandre Marcel, to build a real pagoda in their garden. The architect undertook the project, striving for authenticity. He went so far, some say, as to have the frame made from hand-carved woodwork shipped in from Japan. Madame Morin threw lavish parties here. The couple would show up dressed as emperor and empress. But poor Monsieur Morin couldn't keep up the game. The very year of the grand opening, his wife left him for an associate's son! What a great scenario for a movie! That's probably why since 1930 the doors of the Pagoda have been open to cinema fans. A cinematic temple devoted to showing art and experimental films, the theater is undoubtedly the most exotic in Paris.

🕐 *Depends on which film you want to see*
🍂 *During the Paris monsoon*
♡ *Give the cold shoulder to your associate's son*

5

Thirst Quenchers

C onnoisseurs of pleasure and seekers of the romantic will discover that the streets of the capital offer innumerable delightful places to dip those lips. Here is a selection of our favorite watering holes. Whether you're out for sweetened or unsweetened, tall drinks or short drinks, served in antique Belle Époque coffee cups or in tiny typically Parisian street-cafés' modern stemware, you'll surely find something to your heart's desire.

Le Baiser Salé

1st arrondissement
58, rue des Lombards – Tel. 01 42 33 37 71
Métro Châtelet

What an intriguing and inspirational name -literally, "the salty kiss". On the ground floor, the great U-shaped bar opens its arms to welcome you and give you a peck on both cheeks, French style! But you may find that kisses taste differently on the dance floor when the joint starts hopping. Around 11:00 PM Salsa, African and Latino jazz, and other soulful rhythms spice up the atmosphere. The mix of musical styles and colors forms a palette of kisses from every corner of the planet. Order cool fruity cocktails to refresh your blistered lips. *Bon voyage* into the land of the *baiser salé*. Just a word of warning, though, this delicious musical destination can put a serious dent in your wallet.

🕓 *Every evening until 6:00 AM*
❄ *Snowy or frosty winter nights*
♥ *You won't fog up the windows, the place is already extremely smoky!*

Le Fumoir

1st arrondissement
6, rue de l'Amiral-de-Coligny – Tel. 01 42 92 00 24
Métro Louvre

All in black, Le Fumoir faces the Louvre Museum. Ah, the flicker of candlelight on the tables! The scent of jasmine and Earl Grey in shiny black teapots wafts through the air. You move to the rear of the bar, back near the bookcase, to whisper your sweet nothings.

The large lamp on the windowsill puts an added glow in this romantic moment. Lovely old-fashioned woodwork to make the décor very special. And old-fashioned wood games to pass the time between gentle pecks and other lovers' games. Your waking appetites will appreciate chasing the games with a creamy carrot and ginger soup, then grilled perch with herbs... Yummy!

☺ *Whether for tea or for a late dinner, a great place to linger*

♟ *A table by the window lets you watch snugly-wrapped couples stroll by*

♥ *The perfect setting!*

Le Temps des Cerises

4th arrondissement
31, rue de la Cerisaie – Tel. 01 42 72 08 63
Métro Sully-Morland

D'Artagnan used to drop in at this old tavern after he had accompanied ladies who frequented the jeweler at the corner of the Rue Charles V and the Rue Beautreillis. Amazingly, the jewelry store is still there. But what was the origin of Le Temps des Cerises (literally, cherry season)? It dates back to a time when a cherry orchard formed part of the old cloister of the Célestins, only a few steps away. Today, Gérard—who's got an impressive moustache—and Marie-Claire love their little neighborhood bistro. Every day, there is a festive village atmosphere around the old carved wooden bar, while, hiding in a back corner, couples tease each other beneath an old poster, The Loves of the Gods. Around them, the walls are covered with the photographs of major figures who have spent time sipping drinks here: Robert Doisneau, Raymond Devos, Maxime Le Forestier, to name but a few. And these days the old song is still being hummed by the gentle, anonymous ghosts from work-a-day Paris. One verse touts the anticipated arrival of the fruit in the neighborhood. Hurrah for cherry season! Come join the celebration! Special thanks to Juliette Greco, Yves Montand, Charles Trenet, and many others singers who put the song into our hearts. "Mocking-birds 'n' nightingales, all festive and gay, and beautiful women who laugh and play; while lovers who sit apart radiate sunshine from their heart!"

🕐 *7:45 AM–8:00 PM (it's nice to cuddle all day long)*

🍒 *During cherry season, of course!*

♡ *You won't be the first*

Tea at the Mosque

5th arrondissement

39, rue Geoffroy-Saint-Hilaire – Tel. 01 43 31 18 14

Métro Censier-Daubenton

Believers and atheists, lovers and married folks, nothing prevents you (since it's not a sin) from sampling the three teas at the Paris Mosque. No point in campaigning against alcoholism here. This is teetotalers paradise! As to be expected, no alcohol is served in the mosque tearoom. It is customary to drink three glasses... of tea, that is. The first is bitter, like life. The second (which will be of primary interest to you) is as strong as love. The third and last sneaks up on you, just like death. To be savored with a Middle Eastern pastry. The moment will be sweet and soulful. Just like your lips!

🕐 *2:00 PM to 11:00 PM*

☼ *In the heat of July*

♥ *You're in the heart of a religious monument*

An Intellectual Kiss at Les Deux Magots

6th arrondissement

6, place Saint-Germain-des-Prés – Tel. 01 45 48 55 25

Métro Saint-Germain-des-Prés

In the 1950s, Simone de Beauvoir and Jean-Paul Sartre would come to this café to write for two hours every day. Follow in their footsteps: dedicate two hours regularly to jotting down your sensations after a kiss at Les Deux Magots. You'll notice how your impressions change from one day to the next. In case of writer's block, try repeating the experience! Then have your co-author read your composition and compare notes. Describing a kiss is always amusing, especially when contrasting two points of view. You are not the first poets to come here in search of their muse: Verlaine, Rimbaud, and Mallarmé loved to meet here long before the days of André Breton or Robert Desnos.

🕐 *5:00 PM to 8:00 PM*
🍂 *When drizzle splatters the windowpanes*
♡ *Afterwards analyze it and wax philosophical*

Les Gaufres

6th arrondissement
Luxembourg Gardens
RER station Luxembourg

Le chalet des Gaufres (the waffle chalet) is like a great family saga. The ancestors of the owner here probably sugared the waffles that our grandparents enjoyed when they were tiny tots frolicking in the Luxembourg Gardens. Wiping the powdered sugar off your whitened lips always brings a silly giggle! Hearing the unmistakable scraping of the khaki-colored metal chairs and tables over the gravel terrace brings to mind other romantic moments spent at this charming tea salon. There was a time, perhaps, when only waffles were served here, but today a much wider selection is available for you to choose from. Feeling salacious? How about a salad? For dessert, though, dip your lips in the delicious white powder on the traditional sugared waffles served here.

🕐 *2:00 PM to 5:00 PM*
🍂 *For a table on the terrace*
♥ *Just like Grandpa and Grandma*

The Oldest Café in Paris, Le Procope

6th arrondissement
13, rue de l'Ancienne-Comédie – Tel. 01 40 46 79 00
Métro Odéon

Founded in 1669 (an erotic year...), Le Procope is the granddaddy of Paris cafés. Francesco Procopio dei Coltelli, a gentleman from Palermo, opened a bar in Paris where customers could enjoy a new beverage: coffee. Consequently, no need to spend hours wondering what you might like to drink. The Salon Jean de la Fontaine, on your right as you enter, remains true to the author's "fabled" friendly animals... Delightful friends invited into this abode. You might prefer the table at the back of the café, next to the old books. Books belong here—after all, the Procope was also the world's first literary café. The greats of French literature have frequented the establishment over the centuries. Diderot's *Encyclopedia* was conceived here. Do history and literature make you hungry? Ask for one of the four tables up on the balcony. You can have a quiet lunch upstairs beneath a red parasol.

🕐 *Late morning*

☼ *So you can enjoy the balcony*

♥ *In the salon, Jean de la Fontaine's portrait is staring at you*

L'Atmosphère

10th arrondissement

49, rue Lucien-Sampaix – Tel. 01 40 38 09 21

Métro Jacques-Bonsergent

This charming Paris bistro beside the Canal Saint-Martin has plenty of ambiance, or "*Atmosphère!*" to quote a famous line from a 1930s French film that every self-respecting French person knows and adores, *Hôtel du Nord* by Marcel Carné. If you love places where you can squeal, "Oh, it's so typically Parisian!" you'll certainly like this bar. The décor is retro and nostalgic: charming old wooden bistro chairs, a metal-topped counter, and plenty of Parisian ambiance. It's a neighborhood joint with regulars who stop by for a pint, an expresso, a *pastis*, or just a moment of relaxation. Nothing too fancy, nobody too chic. The kind of bar you'd see in a classic French flick. The kind of bar where working-class Parisians drop by anytime of the day for a change of *atmosphère*. A table suited for lovers like

you is placed right by the window. What a great view of the canal!
Then again, you might prefer a table at the back with an uphol-
stered banquette just right for cuddling.
🕓 *Afternoon*
🍫 *Enjoy a cup of hot chocolate*
♡ *Nobody will mind or hardly notice*

La Guinguette Pirate

12th arrondissement
Port de la Gare, Quai François-Mauriac
(on the river in front of the National Library)
Tel. 01 53 61 08 49
Métro Quai-de-la-Gare

Embark with your lady on a pirate café on a Chinese junk! Unbridle
your passions while imbibing rum before you get on to more serious
business. While firmly anchored at the Quai François Mauriac, careful
not to get sloshed at this Parisian port of call on the Seine. "Made
in China" or "maiden in China?" In any case, admire the china-doll
features of your lovely maiden. Your hearts will be beating like the
thumping of sea waves on a wooden hull. You are already feeling
woozy from the rocking of the boat. Suddenly, the big gun takes aim
at you. Powered up and puckered up, she has you in her sights. Those
lips are ready to attack any minute now. Disarmed, you start to
blush! Take heart, mate! Bottoms up! Hoist the sail!
🕓 *The midnight sun. Avoid weekends*
🌸 *The captivating scent of wood is heightened on muggy July
evenings*
♡ *Play stowaways in the hold!*

Le Lapin Agile

18th arrondissement
22, rue des Saules – Tel. 01 46 06 85 87
Métro Lamarck-Caulaincourt

Close your eyes and use a little imagination. You nearly hear the
chirping of cicadas. Then you blink twice before realizing this isn't
a green-shuttered farmhouse in Provence, no, non, you're on

Montmartre in Paris. Still, you've got it made in the shade, the shade of an acacia tree, that is. Plus the Montmartre vineyards stretch out just to your left, giving an added Provençal illusion. A quarter past eight, it's not too late! At 9:00 PM, the sun starts to go down and the evening twilight begins. Inside there is a festive atmosphere of singing and laughter, poetry and limericks. This monument of Parisian cabarets, Le Lapin Agile, was once run by Adèle, a former French cancan dancer. Alphonse Allais frequented the place as well as the painter André Gill, who completely redecorated it. He made a sign with a rabbit popping out of a saucepan, holding a bottle. Clients of the establishment, including Max Jacob, André Salmon, Roland Dorgelès and poet Apollinaire, were in the habit of calling the cabaret "Le Lapin à Gill" (Gill's Rabbit), which then naturally became "Le Lapin Agile" (the agile rabbit).

☺ *8:15 PM for the cabaret show*
❦ *When the clusters of grapes are ripe*
♡ *It is not every day you get to kiss in a Montmartre cabaret*

La Flèche d'Or

20th arrondissement
102, rue de Bagnolet – Tel. 01 43 72 04 23 or 01 43 72 42 44
Métro Alexandre-Dumas

Call it the "Golden Arrow" if you like. One step inside and you'll feel Cupid's arrow pierce your heart. You'll fall in love with the unique decor and fabulous view of the now abandoned circular railway line. This old railway station smacks of farewell kisses, but say hello to a café that really rocks! Suspended above the bar, in a sawed-off locomotive is the conductor of this jive station: a beer-sipping DJ who always makes sure his tracks are running on time. His music may be wild to some, but it does allow couples who want to hook up to boogie on up to each other. On some evenings, you can see Olive Oil give Popeye a smackeroo in old super-8 films shown on a restroom wall. A smashing place for night owls!

☺ *After 5:00 PM, above the railway*
♨ *The crowd will warm you up*
♡ *No fuss here!*

6

Kisses à la Carte

H ere is a hearty sampling of restaurants, each oozing with romance, to satisfy the most ravenous of appetites. Discriminating gourmets of fine kissing will also be tickled pink. It's common knowledge that when you're in love, you don't count pennies. That's why you won't find any prices listed here. But poor boys need not worry, none of the listings is too expensive.

Jules Restaurant

1st arrondissement

62, rue Jean-Jacques-Rousseau – Tel. 01 40 28 99 04

Métro Les Halles

To which restaurant in Paris should you take your little jewel? Chez Jules, naturally! Located on a little street in the Halles quarter, this restaurant naturally features celebrities named "Jules" which make this place increasingly popular. Besides Julius Caesar, you'll find the mugs of Jules Dassin, Jules Raimu, and Jules Romains, among others. Which table should you reserve? Naturally, the upstairs table beneath the poster of the famous movie *Jules et Jim*. On tonight's menu: the house foie gras, and the spicy sardine and olive tapanades. Your lovey-ducky certainly won't turn up his nose at a *canard sauvage aux herbes* with turnips. Finish your meal with an original desert created by… Léo, the chef's second son. Now what is his first son's name? Oh, you've guessed it!

🕑 *For dinner*

🌣 *Divine summertime veggies*

♥ *You're not alone in wishing you were alone!*

Au Vieux Paris d'Arcole

4th arrondissement

24, rue Chanoinesse – Tel. 01 40 51 78 52

Métro Cité

As Paul Claudel would have said, "extravagant wisteria vines interlace and intertwine" on the wall of the Vieux Paris d'Arcole. Flowers grow in profusion on the sidewalk: geraniums, roses, azaleas, and little mauve bellflowers ringing in the dinner hour. There is a subdued atmosphere in the restaurant dining room from the small violet, red and yellow stained-glass windows. Built on the l'île de la Cité during the 16th century, this unusual old mansion was part of the 37 clergy homes that once surrounded Notre-Dame. This house has seen them come and go! Enjoy the chef's selection of fine wines with specialties of the Aveyron region: *tripoux*, stuffed goose's neck... Quick! Grab your sweetheart's before your sweetheart takes a nibble at yours!

🕐 *Lunch time*

✿ *When floral scents waft through the open door*

♥ *Don't shock the ghosts of the canons who once lived here*

La Charlotte de l'Isle

4th arrondissement
24, rue Saint-Louis-en-l'Île – Tel. 01 43 54 25 83
Métro Pont-Marie

In this unusual tearoom, two cozy picturesque rooms are decorated like a doll house. Everything is tiny! Even the cream for your tea is served in a miniature cruet scarcely larger than a thimble. La Charlotte en l'Isle is a magical kingdom for big and little children. And Tanti, who calls the tune, cooks up succulent poetry in her kitchen! "You, my child, see things so clearly, know how to dream, can fly on a cloud, let me show you my own childlike heart. Sometimes I find myself in a reverie in this little corner of heaven, and I wonder if we are not the same age. Won't you join me on this isle of delights?"

Twice is better than once! Especially once you've savored the *florentin farfelu* or the spice cake. It's no secret that Tanti's kitchen is tempting, too. Take a peek. This is where she conjures up sumptuous, creamy-dreamy chocolate treats. In the back, you'll find a little court with a lovely fountain. An inviting place to taste your partner's chocolate-smudged lips. Waste not, want not!

🕐 *Open only Thursday-Sunday, 2:00 PM to 8:00 PM*

💃 *Need I say why?*

♡ *Sometimes chocolate can be sticky!*

Place du marché Sainte-Catherine

4th arrondissement

Métro Saint-Paul

This charming cobbled-stone outdoors food market recalls vacation spots in the South of France. The main attraction on this voyage are four benches beneath a stand of trees. On all sides of the square are the gaily-lit and colorful terraces of café-restaurants. Banana-yellow tables and chairs at the Côté Soleil restaurant. Cucumber green at the Bistrot de la Place. Red and yellow polka dots at Le Marché (that's actually the name of one of the restaurants). The scents wafting from the Korean barbecue house will whet your appetite. Try the house salad—Webb lettuce, soy sprouts, tomatoes, green and red peppers—, a light vegetable crêpe casserole, or enjoy a basket of shrimp *beignets*. All this will fortify you with vitamins and will put a twinkle in the eyes of all you *catherinettes* (i.e., twenty-something ladies still unmarried by the Feast of Saint Catherine on November the 25th).

☾ *Sunrise or sundown*

☼ *Skimpy summer clothes for outdoors dining*

♡ *Don't be shy about enjoying forbidden fruits*

Le Fogon Saint-Julien

5th arrondissement

10, rue Saint-Julien-le-Pauvre – Tel. 01 43 54 31 33

Métro Saint-Michel

Nibbling delicious *tapas* with a good cocktail in hand can be compared to the delightful business of nibbling your partner's pretty neck before moving on to more serious matters. The Spanish word *tapas* comes from the verb meaning to cover—so cover your lover with kisses! After having lingered over these exquisite delights, move on to a steaming *paella* placed in the center of the table between the two of you. The rice is seasoned and colored with cuttlefish ink. Shell a lobster tail and gently pop it into your sweetheart's sweet little mouth. Finger-licking good! The only minus of the place is that the table has a panel that prevents any possibility of playing footsie. Looks like after dinner you'll have to make up for this shortcoming with a long, romantic stroll along the banks of the Seine.

☺ *Make a reservation for 9:30 PM*

🍁 *Enjoy the autumn leaves and colors around Notre-Dame*

♥ *A classy restaurant, but not much elbow room. The tables are terribly close together*

Le Kiosque Flottant de Notre-Dame

5th arrondissement
Quai de Montebello – Tel. 01 43 54 19 51
Métro Saint-Michel

On certain evenings, when this flatboat restaurant is docked at the Quai de Montebello, a saxophonist sets the tone. Welcome on board! The table at the back of the boat is reserved for you. Sitting in a romantic tête-à-tête, sink your tongues into a summer ice (your choice of pear, pineapple, strawberry) or the *kiosque flottant* (strawberry, lime, coconut, curaçao). The exhilarating night air takes hold of you. Who knows? Maybe your companion will do the same thing later in the evening. For the moment, the party looks promising as it reaches cruising speed, although the boat remains docked at quay. You will have ample time to enjoy the charm of Notre-Dame aglow in a mantle of light.

☺ *Between midnight and 2:00 AM, dessert outside. Café-concert*

✿ *On the deck*

♡ *Night shrouds you*

Les Degrés de Notre-Dame

5th arrondissement
10, rue des Grands-Degrés – Tel. 01 55 42 88 88
RER station Saint-Michel–Notre-Dame or Métro Maubert-Mutualité

The old, wrought iron hotel-restaurant sign could not have ended up in a better spot: two birds under a bed peck at a cluster of grapes in a fruit basket. It seems to be a well-known spot for those in love. A little table in the corner, to the right of the entrance, is set up just for them. But before the feast begins, try out the terrace. It's ideal for apéritifs and "starters" (shall we say). From here you can admire a typically Parisian view: outdoors booksellers on one side, Notre-Dame on the other.

Check out the menu. How does a duck breast and julienne salad sound to you? The *gratin du poète* and the chocolate marquise in a coffee cream sauce will grab your eye. If the dinner goes as hoped, the hostess will hand you the key to one of the ten rooms above the restaurant. The stairwell is decorated with frescos: views of old Paris, the Bois de Boulogne, the Eiffel Tower. A stairway to heaven and an unforgettable night, indeed!

☺ *From dinner hour (meaning no earlier than 8) till dawn*
🍁 *When autumn leaves chase you from the terrace*
♡ *What a question!*

Lapérouse (the last two private salons of Paris)

6th arrondissement
51, quai des Grands-Augustins – Tel. 01 43 26 68 04
Métro Saint-Michel

Since 1766, couples have had their own private salons: two cozy, five-square-meter rooms, each equipped with a little round table, banquette and mirror. During the Belle Époque, these salons were a haven for illicit couples. Kept ladies found an unconventional use for the mirrors on which they would scratch their names to test the diamonds their lovers gave them. As in any public place, so too at the Maison Lapérouse, black-robed investigators could not legally prowl the premises for incriminating evidence of adultery.

While other public houses once provided private salons, this is the only establishment that has kept them. The red velvet seats are large enough to accommodate cuddling during or after the repast. You won't be interrupted. The maître d'hôtel never enters until you have rung for him. Need more bubbly? Just pull that velvet cord!

A subterranean passageway reportedly connects the Senators' salon with the Senate building. Entering discreetly through the secret passage, senators could rendezvous with their paramours. On a slightly more conventional note, marriages are consummated in these chambers, as are second honeymoons or "pilgrimages of love" after 40 or 50 years of marital bliss. Colette, George Sand, Alfred de Musset, Guy de Maupassant, Victor Hugo, Émile Zola, even Alexandre Dumas have all preceded you. A jealously guarded but celebrated address!

☺ *Little matter when! It's the spirit of abandon that counts*

🍷 *When house wines, champagne and cognac are brought out*

♡ *Specially designed for it!*

Le Train Bleu

12th arrondissement
Gare de Lyon – Tel. 01 43 43 09 06
Métro Gare-de-Lyon

Don't miss Le Train Bleu! Its colorful name brings back memories of the mythic luxury express that linked Paris with the French Riviera. The sumptuous décor is classified as a historical monument. But, as the renowned culinary critic Curnonsky reminds us, "You don't go to a restaurant to eat the curtains!" So order the *assiette gourmande du Président*. But which president? Pierre Mendès-France, François Mitterrand and Jacques Chirac have all dined here! Grilled *foie de veau* with onion *confiture* or grilled *petit coquelet Val-de-Saône* with devil's sauce? Nothing like it to put a little fire into your lips! What's for dessert? You'll be babbling for years about the *Baba Christian Guy à la crème fraîche*, created in homage to the renowned chronicler of gastronomy who had his own regular table. Another grand culinary critic, Courtine, confirms this: "I dined here with Christian Guy, a heart of gold, but what a big mouth! And he kept it wide open to gobble up the *baba* that still bears his name. I also supped with Francis Amunategui, chronicler of B. Foyot's veal cutlet (on the menu as well)." The lovely Réjane was spotted in the company of playwright Edmond Rostand, not to mention Colette with the Marquise de Morny.

☺ *7:00 to 9:00 PM, before night trains depart*

🍷 *On your way to a winter weekend in Venice*

♥ *Stick to digestive matters, consoling yourself with thoughts about the joys of night train sleepers.* Bon voyage!

Les Phinéas

14th arrondissement
99, rue de l'Ouest – Tel. 01 45 41 33 50
Métro Pernety

This location is both adorable and original. Original because the menu is slipped into comic books. Among your choices of featured comix heroes are the brave Michel Valiant, Tintin the intrepid, and Astérix the valorous. This charming cast of characters also plays a part in the interior design. You have to launch a veritable attack pushing through the crowd to reach the back of the restaurant. Set your sights on the pirate flag on the wall—definitely the best place for general fooling around. Red theater curtains offer a stage for the heroes that you are this evening. But before you start bubbling like champagne, choose your table carefully. The place is packed with lovers in intimate tête-à-têtes at cozy tables, their figures silhouetted by little lamps. Catch a *filet de mérou* (grouper) as it passes by on a bed of curried vegetables. Also try the fabulous main-course pies. With a little imagination, and a slight turn of the head, no doubt you will spot comic-book hero Gaston Lagaffe with the exquisitely charming Mademoiselle Jeanne. For dessert, Les Phinéas offers you the possibility to order personalized cakes on the theme of your choice.

🕐 *10 PM to 11 PM. Avoid the lunch time crowd*

🔥 *The old stove will warm your hearts*

♡ *Long kisses are a must because the service can be a bit slow, especially when you have to wait for the cook to go to the bakery for more bread… at 10:30 PM*

Le Ciel de Paris

Tour Montparnasse, 56th floor
15th arrondissement – Tel. 01 40 64 77 64
Métro Montparnasse-Bienvenüe

Go ahead! Shoot for the stars! Tonight anything is possible! Le Ciel de Paris Restaurant will put all Paris at your feet. Located on the 56th floor of the Montparnasse tower, it offers you a panoramic view of the city of lights. It's the tops in gastronomic delights. The *bisque de homard à l'anis* will put stars in your eyes. And the *croustillant de pétoncles* with its tomato-orange-avocado dressing will put you on cloud nine. If, after all these gourmet delights, you actually manage to lift your face up from your plate, you will no doubt fall under the spell of your bewitching dinner mate—as splendid as the million shimmering lights of Paris. Take a tip from us, reserve a table slightly away from the windows. The view is much better.

☺ *From sunset to the middle of the night*

✿ *Keep your heads out of the clouds*

♡ *Didn't come all this way up for nothin', right?*

Le Bistro des Dames

17th arrondissement
18, rue des Dames – Tel. 01 45 22 13 42
Métro Place-de-Clichy

Shhh! Don't tell a soul, but we know of a secret passageway that a girlfriend of ours discovered on one her dates when she went to powder her nose. The main dining room at Le Bistro des Dames simply seemed far too banal—obviously a cover-up for something special, something extraordinary. She found it, all right! Go see for yourself. Tiptoe to the back and get a peek at the pretty hidden garden. It's only open when weather permits. The verandah will then be awash with sunshine. An exquisite address for lunch. At the far end of the garden is the very charming Hôtel Eldorado, all sung under the branches of a magnificent tree around which pretty little tables and folding chairs are arranged. This restaurant and wine bar is oozing with charm, and the service is very friendly. Lap it all up!

☺ *Lunch (practically feels like you're on a picnic)*

✿ *Mussels as a starter on the terrace?*

♡ *Otherwise, why bother searching high and low for a hideaway as fab' as this? Afterward lunch, the gorgeous little hotel beckons you to drop in for a summer siesta...*

Chez Plumeau

18th arrondissement
4, place du Calvaire – Tel. 01 46 06 26 29
Métro Abbesses or Anvers, then funicular or stairs

A honeymoon in Paris without Plumeau's honey crêpe would be like a wedding without a cake. Savor it on the evening terrace during a full moon... Gather the nectar from her honey-filled lips. To die for! It's all the happiness that we could wish newlyweds on their honeymoon to Montmartre. This evening, the queen bee and her best "worker" will take shelter beneath a leafy rooftop amidst a swarm of kisses. After a few honey crêpes, you'll find an inviting little bench beneath some trees where you can cuddle. But don't overdo it: you just might get stung.

🕐 *At dinner one evening when the moon is full*
🌼 *Just after the wedding season*
♡ *More than ever*

Le Moulin de la Galette

18th arrondissement
83, rue Lepic – Tel. 01 46 06 84 77
Métro Abbesses or Lamarck-Caulaincourt

The early 19th century Debray mill was a farm and inn where Parisians would come for a *galette* (a sort of pancake) washed down with a bowl of fresh milk. In 1876, with pretty girls sitting at garden tables, Renoir created the immense and colorful canvas of the *Moulin de la Galette* with joyous brush strokes. The place had become a popular dance hall by Renoir's time. Montmartre dressmakers' apprentices came here to rendezvous, chaperoned (or not) by doting mothers. Every Sunday afternoon, the girls would swirl to polkas and mazurkas with neighborhood lads. However, today, the clientele is quite well-heeled. White tablecloths and red velvet highlight the decor. The menu includes items such as filet mignon of lamb or grilled trout with rosemary. This address is a must for Montmartre lovers.

🕐 *Sunday evening after the last dance*
🕊 *For a* galette *fit for a king*
♥ *Numerous posters of deceased chanteuse Dalida ogling you*

With My Honey-True at Patachou!

18th arrondissement
9, place du Tertre – Tel. 01 42 51 06 06
Métro Abbesses or Anvers, then funicular or stairs
Peek into the shop window of chocolate and ice-cream maker Patachou. You'll feel overwhelmed by the beauty and grandeur of Paris, capital of gastronomy. Plus, the panoramic view from this address is truly exceptional. If you're feeling warm, enjoy the terrace and take a load off your feet. Try their méli-mélo! Scrumptious!

☕ *For tea time*
🎋 *Beat the throngs of tourists*
♡ *And even more*

La Maroquinerie, Literary Café

20th arrondissement
23, rue Boyer – Tel. 01 40 33 30 60
Métro Gambetta (take the Place Martin-Nadaud exit)
Keep the noise down, no loud smackeroos! There is a reading tonight at La Maroquinerie. This refurbished 19th century factory in the 20th arrondissement has undergone quite a transformation. It has donned an evening gown and will dine only on food-for-thought and such refined delicacies. On the menu today: watercress salad with shrimp and lime, served in the central courtyard.

Feast your eyes on the luxurious greenery and pretty garden furniture. Then feast on the braised *pintade aux choux rouges*, a *plat de résistance* that nobody can resist. The clatter of dishes harmonizes with the music played by guest bands and the poetry readings. Truly unique.

☕ *Chic in the evening, laid-back in the afternoon*
🎋 *When literary salons blossom in Paris courtyards*
♡ *Inspired by dramatic readings, of course!*

7

Kissing Benches
Kissing Binges

n expert in the field, the popular French singer Georges Brassens in a perky well-known tune glorified *"les bancs publics"*—park and street benches where lovers sit and kiss, not giving a hoot what passersby think. Warning! The City of Paris park authority demands decorum, decency, and order in parks and other public places. You will have to juggle between what the law allows and what your raging hormones dictate. Take a tip from Paris high-school kids. Observe what happens on street benches after school lets out. You will agree, those kids are definitely on a kissing binge! Need we remind you that Paris benches belong to France's national heritage and the art of expressing young love?

Jardin des Tuileries

1st arrondissement

Métro Tuileries or Concorde

Throughout history, the Tuileries Garden has always attracted wayward lovers. Aristocrats, bourgeois, poor people, hetero- and homosexuals, prostitutes... all have played their roles in making this a lovers' garden. It was so highly appreciated by Parisians of the 18th century that when torrential rains closed the Tuileries, lovers fretted and whimpered outside the locked gates. In the 19th century, husbands and wives would stroll in arm-and-arm at the north gate, then quickly slip away from each other to join their lovers at the south gate. Today, lovebirds rendezvous around the ponds, or on the dark green benches, near waffle vendors. Today, the Jardin des Tuileries remains a favorite cruising area for gays. And so the garden continues its historic mission: satisfaction for lovers of all stripes.

🕒 *From 3:00 to 5:00 PM*

⛸ *Outdoors ice-skating*

♥ *Since the days of Catherine de Médicis*

Place des Vosges

4th arrondissement

Métro Bastille, Chemin-Vert or Saint-Paul

Victor Hugo, head of the Romantic school, occupied the second floor of No. 6 on the square between 1832 and 1848. He wrote *Les Misérables* there. Marion Delorme, heroine of one of his dramas but also mistress of Condé and Richelieu, lived at No. 11. Bossuet lived at 17, Richelieu at 21, Madame de Sévigné at 61, and Théophile Gautier and Alphonse Daudet at No. 8. These famed names spent a good bit of time in the garden below. But which bench did they prefer? Perhaps it was the bench opposite No. 7 Place des Vosges, near the gate. It is ideally located for listening to weekly Sunday afternoon concerts given by a little philharmonic group beneath the arcades. This romantic bench will set your heart vibrating like violin strings.

☺ *After 2:00 PM on Sundays*

❀ *While it's raining, to enhance the melancholy of the violins*

♡ *Take a quick look around in case Monsieur Hugo is peering out his window*

Square Barye

4th arrondissement

Pont de Sully

Métro Sully-Morland

Watch the boats passing on the Seine while you slurp on a Berthillon ice… You'll have tasted bliss! This happiness is to be found at the end of the Square Barye where five benches are embedded for eternity at the tip of the Île Saint-Louis. To your right on the Quai Saint-Bernard, the silhouettes of outdoor sculptures rise high into the air. Straight ahead, the elevated metro rumbles over the Pont d'Austerlitz. On sunny summer days, the Quai de Béthune is jammed with sun-bathers soaking up rays. On rainy autumn evenings, weeping willows dip their frail branches into the Seine. And when winter winds blast, kisses flutter through the air from bridge to bridge.

☺ *Outside after 10:00 PM*

❀ *Plant a kiss on those sweet lips and watch love grow*

♡ *You reap what you sow*

Love as Mighty as a Cedar at the Jardin des Plantes

5th arrondissement

Métro Jussieu or Censier-Daubenton

A little stone bench embraces the trunk of a magnificent cedar of Lebanon. A mighty metaphor for your own tender embrace. Wrap your arms around each other. What could make you happier? High up in the branches, two pigeons bill and coo. Bliss is contagious! We can thank Bernard Jussieu who, in 1734, according to legend, carried the seeds of this cedar in his hat. From the vantage point of this tree you'll see the belvedere of the Jardin des Plantes. A lovers' lane leads to this dovecote from which love takes flight. The view from the belvedere is breathtaking and splendid.

☺ *Between 5:00 and 6:00 PM*

☼ *Flower power!*

♥ *Birds do it! Bees do it! So let's fall in love!*

The Luxembourg Gardens and the de Médicis Fountain

6th arrondissement

RER station Luxembourg

The Duchess de Berry, the regent's daughter, spent summer nights in the garden in the company of daring suitors. But nowadays the garden paths are only open during daylight. Daytime lovers can hide among the trees surrounding the de Médicis fountain. Graceful statues here represent characters from Greek mythology such as the sea-nymph Galatea in the arms of her youthful lover, Acis. Galatea —"the milk white" and mythological mother of the Gauls—was running from a jealous husband, Polyphemus, an uncouth Cyclops. This sensuous work of art caused much heated debate, exciting the passions of the most prudish souls. Soon after the sculpture had been placed in the fountain, a jealous fool splashed the shimmering whiteness of lovely Galatea's body with ink.

☺ *Nippy early morning hours*

❄ *In the frosty pathways among the statues*

♥ *Watch out for jealous one-eyed husbands!*

A Novel Idea!

6th arrondissement
Square Gabriel-Pierné (corner of Rue Mazarine and Rue de Seine)
Métro Odéon

The storybook-like Square Gabriel-Perné, invites you to come up with an original idea to charm your young lady or gent. A love story, naturally! Recite a ballad about a prince and dame wooing, just like you, on an open book sculpted in stone. Then improvise! Recount that yours was "a chance meeting by the side of the road"... Better still, imagine the two of you as the heroes of a passionate love story in this "city of 100,000 novels," as Balzac put it. For those of you who are less imaginative, try standing on the bench then belt out your favorite love song. "This will be an everlasting love" will certainly do. A 1968 statue by Marcelio Tommasy, with the pretty name of Carolina, graces the square. Careful! Carolina's sexy swerve of the hips might knock you right off that bench.

🕓 *At the dawn of a love story*
🌸 *Ah! the promise of spring!*
♡ *As in any novel*

Sins of Babylon

7th arrondissement
Jardins Catherine-Labouré – 33, rue de Babylone
Métro Sèvres-Babylone

It hardly resembles Babylon! Quite the contrary! This square, which was rechristened Jardin Catherine-Labouré (canonized in 1947) was formerly a nuns' vegetable patch. So, for heaven's sake, watch your manners! Today, instead of tomatoes, carrots, and leeks, there are apple trees, cherry trees, and hazelnut trees. The garden is now a veritable orchard and children can enjoy playing on the green grass. On beautiful summer days, red gingham tablecloths spread out beneath the shade of fruit trees. Picnics on the lawn are quite popular in season. Ambassadors' wives (you are in that part of the city) stroll with their children... pint-sized budding bureaucrats. A number of large bushes provide shelter for romantic interludes. At the other end of the garden, looking up through the boughs of a linden tree, you can thank the heavens above for Babylon!

🕓 *Between noon and 2:00 PM*

🍎 *Fruit trees in blossom, all white and pink*

♡ *Lazing on the lawn*

Bois de Vincennes

12th arrondissement

Métro Porte-Dorée or Château-de-Vincennes

Little boats glide through the morning mist, while you in your jogging suit huff and puff trying to compete with junior joggers in a lap around the lake. Ah, fiddlesticks! Take a breather near the waterfall! Still can't catch your breath? Too proud to let on about it to the one who dragged you out of that cozy bed? Then fake a hypoglycemia attack. Demand the mouth-to-mouth resuscitation that you deserve. You won't be refused because the area lends itself more to cuddling than to Olympic exploits. While closing your eyes for a moment, you will think you've been transported out into the countryside. An artificial countryside, of course, but one of those rare, remote wooded areas without the din of Paris traffic.

🕓 *At the crack of dawn when the rooster crows!*

🥾 *Pretend you're lost babes in the woods*

♡ *Mouth-to-mouth*

Looking for Love at the Parc Montsouris

14th arrondissement

RER station Cité-Universitaire

The very day it was inaugurated, all the water drained out of the manmade lake at Parc Montsouris due to an embarrassing construction error. If you're high and dry—love-wise—there is no need to be embarrassed about being here all alone! It's a great place to meet your next love interest. A favorite pick-up place for girls and boys! After you've found your little treasure, lead him or her beneath the twist of beech tree branches. You don't have to beat around the bush... because this is a tree. An added little tease, head over to the Bonbonnière, the park's concession stand, and treat your new-found love to chocolate, strawberry, praline, or pistachio ice cream... Then suggest strolling over to the little carousel of pink wooden horses and pigs.

☺ *Before school lets out, no long lines at the concession stand!*

✿ *Because of the strawberry ice cream*

♡ *Especially beneath the twisted beech tree branches*

Young Love at La Cité Universitaire

14th arrondissement
37, boulevard Jourdan
RER station Cité-Universitaire

In the heart of "Cité U", intertwined and lolling on the grass sweet nothings are whispered in young ears. Youssef, a mathematics major, runs his fingers through Petula's shimmering hair and sings her something like: "For you, my princess, I will braid my love into your curly blonde locks. Such vows, my dear, will make you cruel to all other lovers..." The scene is set! An early-morning serenade beneath the arcades. Later, rap music will be blaring from dormitory windows. Join the academic community to study the art of tender romance. Enter stage left at the theater-in-the-round at No. 37, boulevard Jourdan. And without further ado, on with the show... or rather, on with the kiss!

☺ *Between noon and 2:00 PM*

✿ *October, after a long summer vacation*

♡ *It's appropriate at your age. What do you expect?*

Kisses Down in the Tropics

16ᵉ arrondissement
The greenhouses of Auteuil
1 bis, avenue de la Porte-d'Auteuil
Métro Porte-d'Auteuil

If some slow-talking southerner (from Marseille, for example) tells you a tall tale about having seen gold fish two feet long… believe it! These fish evolved in the pond of one of Auteuil's amazing greenhouses, constructed at the end of the 19th century where Louis XV's tree nursery once stood. The tropical climate unleashes desires for savage, torrid moments. But control yourselves! Jane, calmly take your Tarzan by the hand, and begin an educational tour of the 100 different species growing here: palm trees, tropical Asian hibiscus, coffee shrubs, mango and guava trees, Brazilian Creole tulips. Further away, in an aviary, exotic birds fluff, flutter, and flirt. On a little wooden bridge, a couple of grave lovers engrave their initials in the bark of a gigantic banana tree. Then a shrill whistle puts an end to such excesses and "crimes against Nature," announcing the 7:00 PM closing time. The oasis of love closes its doors to Parisians and… even to visitors from Marseille.

🕐 *Late afternoon*
🔀 *For the change of scenery*
♡ *Go on, Tarzan, show her you're a man!*

Seen and scene at the Bois

16th arrondissement
Bois de Boulogne
Métro Porte-d'Auteuil or Porte-Dauphine – Bus 63, Porte-de-la Muette

"Weddings in the Bois de Boulogne are not performed by priests." This odd 17th-century French saying indicates that the Bois was not then highly recommended as a rendezvous for lovers. On the other hand, during the Second Empire, it was recommended that you should be seen strolling around the lake from 2 to 4 PM in winter and 3 to 6 PM in summer. The emperor and empress were fond of making appearances there. As Impress Eugenie stepped out of her carriage, an imperial bodyguard held back jovial types overly-eager to pay their respects. The emperor, who was not really much for walking, preferred to follow in his carriage, which he drove himself. During the Belle Époque, walks "through the *Bois*" were a must in high society. But the recommended hours had changed. It was an absolute must to be seen there between 11 AM and noon to be reported in the pages of *Le Gaulois*, the official high society journal.

☺ *Weekdays during office hours when joggers are at work. Or weekends when a major soccer game is being shown on TV*

⛸ *Flee the crowds, go for a skate on the frozen lake*

♡ *Darlings, it's a must!*

Well Versed in Love at Le Square des Poètes

16th arrondissement
Entrance Avenue du Général-Sarrail
Métro Porte-d'Auteuil

Molière, Racine, Ronsard, Lamartine, Baudelaire, Mallarmé and many other illustrious poets invite you into their garden. "Come! I shall tell you of things so pure that neither the periwinkle nor pale lily-of-the-valley, hidden beneath the moss, could express it in sweeter words." Just as the other poets, Ernest Fleury exalts nature in his poetry, as seen by these lines engraved on a stele beside a path. Here newlyweds, golden-anniversary and still-unmarried couples come strolling. Numerous benches allow them a chance to take a break (or "caesura" for the poetically inclined). Such a delicate moment was aptly described by Rosemonde Gérard: "A familiar bench, all green with moss, on this bench from long ago we again will come to chat, sharing sweet and tender joy, each phrase sealed with a kiss." What a shame that this dear little departed circle of poets cannot rest in peace. However, this busy traffic circle knows no poetry. Concentrate hard and you may find the missing rhyme for the French word "*poème*." Go ahead, say it! "*Je... t'aime!*"

☺ *Sunday mornings when traffic is calm*

🐝 *and* 🍂 *"There is nothing more beautiful than a flower in April except the golden leaves of autumn." (Fernand Gregh)*

♡ *I dare you to try kissing rhymes!*

Buttonholed at Batignolles

17th arrondissement

At 144, rue Cardinet

Métro Brochant

Making wedding plans but haven't found an appropriate setting yet? Head to Square des Batignolles right away. Take some professional advice on how to achieve a soft focus in your photos: place the bride's stocking tightly over the camera lens. Oops, she's not wearing hosiery? Then ask any lady passing through the garden. If nobody has a stocking to lend, do some mouth-to-mouth to steam up that lens! Lastly, for you ladies, here's a tip which can save your life. If your photographer hasn't show up by nightfall, run (don't walk) to the park exit because bodies of women hacked to pieces have been discovered in the bushes. This teensy-weensy gruesome detail aside, the setting is stunningly romantic. In the spring, birds twitter gaily in the trees, and the blood-red tulips are a *natural* shade of red. However, think twice before kissing a stranger in Batignolles. And, never, never allow a stranger to kiss you on the neck!

☺ *Avoid the park when it's invaded by baby carriages*

🎎 ✿ 🐚 *Wedding season!*

♥ *For the photo!*

Adam and Eve on Vacation in Paris

18th arrondissement

17, rue Saint-Vincent

Métro Lamarck-Caulaincourt

Where would Adam and Eve go if they were visiting Paris? Why, quite naturally to the natural Jardin Saint-Vincent, where the only caretaker is Mother Nature. A garden unlike any other, for only wild plants grow here. The woody nightshade, a creeping plant that slithers like a snake, whispering in your ear that there is forbidden fruit you and your mate should partake. Certainly not celandine, with its pretty violet flowers and yellow stamens, a poisonous plant.

Resist the temptation to pick the wild flowers or take any cuttings for your planters back home. The plants here are strictly off limits to grubby little hands. This little paradise, ideal for awakening love from fallow ground, is only open to nature lovers from April to

October. The gates are open on Mondays from 4:00–6:00 PM and Saturdays 2:00–6:00 PM. The fragile equilibrium of Eden must be preserved.

☺ *As indicated above*

🍀 *Adam and Eve always vacation in spring, when fig leaves sprout*

♡ *Near the little pond*

Make Yourself at Home!

18th arrondissement
Parc de la Turlure
Entrance Rue du Chevalier-de-la-Barre or Rue de la Bonne
Métro Abbesses or Anvers, then funicular or stairs

Above the artificial waterfall in the Parc de la Turlure are what appear to be two couches set at an angle, almost giving you the impression you are in your own living room. But these couches are made of stone. Bad news for creatures of comfort! For others, the intimacy is complete. Unlike nearby Sacré-Cœur with its endless crowds of tourists, this park is often very calm and practically deserted. So, at your leisure, you can stretch out on your couch and place your weary head on your darling's lap. The gorgeous plunging view of Paris is better than television! Good perspectives for a delightful evening ahead. Panoramic!

☺ *Dusk for a gorgeous sunset*

🍀 *At the close of tourist season, when the Montmartre vineyards are ready for harvest*

♡ *Home, sweet home!*

Historic Kiss of Peace

19th arrondissement
Parc des Buttes-Chaumont
Métro Buttes-Chaumont or Botzaris

Thanks to Emperor Napoleon III, the Parc des Buttes-Chaumont welcomes lovers of all sorts. Thanks a mil', Nap'! An admirer of English landscaping, he created this immense park of luscious greenery between 1865 and 1867. Enthusiasts of "back-to-nature" kissing should also thank him for the Parc Montsouris, the Bois de

Boulogne, and the Bois de Vincennes. At the Parc des Buttes-Chaumont the ideal spot for a romantic smooch rises right before your eyes. The park's belvedere sits high atop the hill. It will give you the thrill of vertigo during your kiss. It will also give you the thrill of being in a very historic area of Paris. It was from this high point that on September 30, 1814, Czar Alexander I gave the order to cease combat after seeing Paris in flames and tears. So, if you have had a spat with your pet, cease all hostilities. Place your arms gently round your babe's waist, nuzzle up, and be glad you have this special moment together.

☺ *As late in the day as possible*

🌸 *Celebrate the September 30th cease-fire*

♡ *A kiss of peace should be as long as possible*

8

The Paris Kissing Calendar

T here are many special occasions for kissing all throughout the year. But where and when? Here are the details on a few highly recommended events in Paris.

Late February to early March: Bucolic Kisses
15th arrondissement
Porte de Versailles
Métro Porte-de-Versailles
Feeling a need for fresh air? Do barns full of hay and green pastures inspire you? The annual International Salon of Agriculture provides occasions for having a good time without leaving the capital. Erotic-bucolic pleasures are guaranteed and labeled "terroir de Paris" (produce of Paris). However, you may sorely feel the lack of intimacy in this farm show. Flee the herds! Hide behind a goat, a cow, or a big fat sow!

Late March to early June: Love Apples
12th arrondissement
Bois de Vincennes, Pelouse de Reuilly
Métro Porte-Dorée
The Foire du Trône is a popular Paris fair. Strut like a peacock, spread those tail feathers, and join the line for a ride on the equally colorful Ferris Wheel. You've already got a ticket to ride with the man or lady of your dreams! Soon the two of you will be safely tucked into the bucket and taking off. Lips smacking with cotton candy and candied love apples, you and your lover may not come unglued in time to enjoy the view. Use the tip of your tongue to melt the sugar away. Whoa! The giant wheel's rotating the other way! With a bit o' luck, you might later get another type of exhilarating ride!

Late April: Breathless!
All over Paris
What woman has never dreamed that her man would chase her to the ends of the earth—or at least across town? Step right on up,

gentlemen! Sign up for the Paris Marathon. Join the squad! Instead of running for the sake of merely running, be different, run for a kiss at the finish. Perhaps all the participants will share the same motivation. For novices and those with shortness of breath, the October Paris 20-km run is a good second choice. Until then, remember to train everyday.

June 21: The Longest Kiss Contest
Anywhere in Paris
It's summer equinox, the longest day of the year. Try non-stop kissing until that old sun finally sets.

July 13: Firemen's Ball
18th arrondissement
In front of Square Carpeaux
Métro Guy-Môquet
Firemen really know how to stoke the fires of love! On the night of July 13, one of the hottest dance events in Paris precedes Bastille Day celebrations. Flowery summer dresses sway in rhythm to the java, tango, or accordion classics that Parisians still love to dance to. Lovers burning with passion whisper sweet nothings as they dance a "slow'" then boogie to the hottest hit tunes. Fortunately, the fire station is on alert 24 hours a day! Then again, any fireman worth his salt would probably rather fan the flames in a lady's heart than put out the fire. Paris firemen are world-renown for their great looks, flamboyant uniforms, and rippling muscles. In the 18th arrondissement, the firemen of the Square Carpeaux station lead the dance. A great way for locals to make new acquaintances without ever leaving home turf. The multicolored Chinese lanterns serve as candlelight for new and old couples alike.

July 14: Explosive Kisses
7th arrondissement
At the foot of the Eiffel Tower
Métro Bir-Hakeim
During the Ancien Régime, the kings of France knew how much Parisians loved gigantic fireworks displays. One of the most spectacular on the history books was for the wedding of Louis XIV and

Marie-Thérèse in 1660, in which 250 stars in the sky spelled out the names of the newlyweds. The delirium was just as grandiose for the wedding of Louis XVI and Marie-Antoinette. Your fireworks, too, will explode at the Trocadéro for the Bastille Day celebrations.

Mid-September: Open Doors and Open Hearts
Looking for a monumental kiss? No problem. During the *Journées du Patrimoine* (national heritage days), take advantage of the open doors at any of France's national monuments or government institutions. You can smooch in ministerial offices, at the Senate, at Matignon, or even at the Élysée Palace.

9

Kissing Terms: Choice Morsels

"Like a sermon given up close, a kiss
That fills your spirit is a promise
Or a vow seeking confirmation,
A deep and soulful sensation.
It's a secret in which the mouth becomes the ear
A moment of the infinite which you almost hear,
A communion that tastes like a flower
So the heart might breathe a short hour
Because the soul's pleasure is on the lips!"

Edmond Rostand,
Cyrano de Bergerac, 1898.

"Something like a delicious and passionate fruit
crushed upon the mouth..."

Theuriet,
The Marriage of Gérard, 1875.

"Do you know where your true power comes from? From kissing, from kissing alone. When we know how to offer our lips in abandon, we become like queens. But kissing is only a prelude, a charming introduction more delectable than the work itself. It is a prelude that you will re-read endlessly, while you cannot always... reread the book. Yes, the encounter of lips is the most perfect, the most divine sensation that can be afforded to human beings, the ultimate and furthest limit of happiness. In kissing, and only in kissing, one sometimes feels the impossible union of souls that we yearn for, a stirring mix of yielding hearts [...] This profound sensation is born from a single caress. Two beings have now become one: that is the kiss. Not even the violent delirium of complete possession is equal to the trembling as mouths approach, the first moist, fresh contact, and then the profound attachment, long, so long, of one to the other!"

Guy de Maupassant,
Stories and Novellas, *The Kiss*, 1882.

Our own French Dictionary of Kissing Terms

Almost all French language dictionaries give the same heartless definition for the French term "baiser" (kiss). Unfortunately, the dictionaries strip it of all poetry and render it excessively and dismally technical. It seems it is up to us to put the love back in the term. Let's get right to the point, today's verb not only means to kiss but to make love. Pronouncing it is as easy as doing it: "bezzay." (The "b" is the same as in English. The "ai" is about the same as the "e" in "egg." The "s" buzzes like a "z." And the final "er" is a wee shorter than the "ay" in "okay.")

So what about the other words you learned in your first year of French, like "embrasser" and "bise"? Don't worry, you will find them in our selection, plus a wealth of synonyms and derivative words.

BAISE: noun, feminine. Like most all the derivatives of the verb "*baiser*," this word has a sexual meaning and is considered vulgar. In standard French, it indicates physical lovemaking. Only in certain regions like the North and French-speaking Belgium is it a synonym for an "affectionate little kiss." Use this word carefully!

BAISEMAIN: noun, masculine. Kiss of the hand. Quite common in France during the 16th century, the "*baisemain*" was spoken, but not performed. When taking leave of someone, it was customary to say, "I kiss your hand," or "I kiss your Lordship's hand." First used in 1306 in the feudal context of the vassal-sovereign relationship, today it indicates a gesture of politeness of a man towards a woman. This practice has always been limited to the upper classes in society.

BAISER: noun, masculine. Written around 980 as "*baisair*," noun formed from the verb "*baiser*." The action of applying the lips on one part of a being as a sign of respect, affection or love. According to the *Dictionnaire historique de la langue française*, the noun does not carry the same sexual connotation as the verb (see below), and has preserved the vitality of its original meaning. Modern French uses the combination of "*embrasser-baiser*." In contemporary usage, it competes with "*bise*," "*bisou*" when the context is not erotic.

BAISER: verb. The *Dictionnaire de la langue du XIXe et XXe siècles*, published by France's official national center for scientific research (because all of this is highly scientific), defines the verb as "applying, pressing the lips on some part of the person (notably the mouth, with an active caressing motion, suction, grasping, etc.) or on some object representing the person, in a sign of love." According to the dictionary, the word's origin is from the Latin *basiare* (circa 980), derived from *basium*, first used in an erotic sense along with *osculum*, (literally "little mouth"). It was first used in French in the context of the kiss between Christ and his disciples. Later, in the 12th century romantic context, it was used as an erotic euphemism for "physically possess"—in other words, sexual intercourse. This usage appears during the 16th and 17th centuries, chiefly among Burlesques. But it was ambiguous then, the "decent" meaning being more prevalent. Nevertheless, Molière's line *"Baiserai-je, mon père?"* was already making audiences snicker as it held a double-entendre: "Shall I kiss, father?" "Shall I screw, father?". The erotic meaning led to the replacement of baiser with embrasser to convey the original meaning of simple kissing. Like an innocent kiss, words and acts can take you a long way! In modern French slang, the verb *baiser* (much like its English equivalent) can also mean to swindle, to con, to shaft. Use this word carefully!

BAISER DE JUDAS: noun, masculine. The kiss Judas gave to Christ signified his betrayal. By extension, a traitor's kiss: a demonstration of affection by kissing another while cherishing the hope of obtaining something in return.

BAISER DE LAMOURETTE: noun, masculine. This idiomatic French expression indicates a short-lived reconciliation. Its origin is a reference to the ephemeral agreements between opposing political parties in the 1792 legislative assembly. Abbé Lamourette made a passionate plea for mutual understanding and invited the revolutionaries to make peace with each other.

BAISERET: noun, masculine; obsolete. According to the dictionary of the French language of the 16th century, "*baiseret*" was the diminutive of "*baiser*." Why not declare, like the poet Olivier de Magny: "I do wish that your mouth you would speedily proffer, so as a sweet little kiss to offer." As an obsolete word, there is absolutely no sense in a foreigner trying to place it in a sentence in French, unless of course you aim to impress a certain special someone...

BAISEUR: noun, masculine. According to the dictionary of the French language of the 16th century, it simply refers to someone who gives a kiss. But warning! In modern French, it is a crude and shocking term. It means sexually promiscuous, a great lay, or horny, depending on the context.

BAISOUILLER: verb; slang, crude. To have sex in a mediocre or routine fashion. Aside from the fact that it is nearly impossible for most non-French to pronounce, it should be avoided because it is a very vulgar word.

BEC: noun, masculine. Bird's beak. Derived around 1119 from the Latin *beccus* (beak). By the early 13th century "*bec*" was used to refer to the human mouth in quaint language, and so it remains today. By extension (or metonymy to use a big fancy word), it means face, person, or, especially in Switzerland and Quebec, a peck. The amusing modern slang expression "*laisser quelqu'un le bec dans l'eau*" (literally to leave somebody with his beak in the water) means to leave someone in a lurch. Lastly, there is the old saying, "*Il n'est bon bec que de Paris*" which means that the finest gourmets in France are only to be found in the capital.

BÉCOT: noun, masculine. Derived from "*bec*" with the diminutive suffix "*-ot*." At the end of the 18th century, a familiar equivalent of "*baiser*" from which "*bécotement*" is derived (attested by Flaubert in 1863). Cute, but not at all in use today.

BÉCOTER: verb. To bill and coo. A delightful verb in current usage. Undoubtedly derived from the above term. Try this as a compliment to your favorite kisser: "*Ah, j'aimerais te bécoter partout!*" While it might impress your sweetheart, then again... Just make sure you say it with a heavy accent.

BICHER: verb; familiar. Originating in 19th century dialect and derived from the Latin *beccus* (beak). The expression *"ça biche!"* probably comes from the speech of fishermen crying, "I've got a bite!" Regional usage in Lyons: *"se bichi"* (to nibble or to bite one another). *"Bicher"* means to kiss in certain southeastern dialects. The derivations *"bicheur, bicheuse"* (noun and adjective; m. and f. forms) designate someone who likes to tease.

BIDOU: noun, masculine. What is the art of *"le bidou"*? Lightly brush your partner's lips while closing your eyes and then start again until the pressure of your lips is barely perceptible. A *"bidou"* is simply a slight contact. Withdraw your lips as soon as you have made contact with your partner's lips. No doubt the most frustrating kiss!

BISE: noun, feminine. A smack, a peck, a kiss on the cheek as a greeting. The latter is a major aspect of French culture which causes quite a lot of confusion for the non-French (and even among the French themselves). The typical French invitation for this cordial familiarity is, *"On se fait la bise?"* (How about a peck on the cheek, dear?) Off with the glasses, then you dive in to start left then right, oops, or is it right then left…? Do you think you are psychologically geared up for two pecks on the cheek? Surprise! The other person insists that in their region, family, or circle of friends, it's an obligatory three (left, right, left… or is it right, left, right?). It may likely be four pecks: left, right, left, right… unless its right, left, right, left! Ah, shucks! Just go with the flow, smile and giggle. It'll all turn out fine.

BISOU: noun, masculine. Popular during the 1960s and still popular today, *"bisou"* was already in use in the 1900s. The suffix *"-ou"* tacked on to *"bise"*. The term is particularly used with children. *"Tu me fais un bisou, mon chou?"* (Give me a kiss, sweetie-pie.)

EMBRASSER: verb. To kiss, or to hug. According to one etymological dictionary of the French language, this verb only means to take someone in your arms and hug affectionately. But we all know it is commonly used for to kiss. Compliment your French lover's kissing skills with: *"Mmm, les Français embrassent tellement bien!"*

PELLE: noun, feminine. From the Latin *pala*, spade, more specifically "what one plunges, sinks into..." Get the idea? "*Se rouler une pelle*" is another term for French kissing.

POUTOU: noun, masculine. A word from the southern French langue d'Oc (poudoum, poutoun, poutou), onomatopoeic in origin, a "*pot*," designating the lips, or the "*moue*." Usage is similar to "*bisou*." "*Poutou*" is a familiar term used in certain regions, indicating a friendly kiss, affectionate and resonant. During encounters in Paris, one sometimes hears the derivative "*poutouner*." Among young people, "*poutouner*" consists of blowing on your partner's skin and making the lips vibrate to emit a sound.

ROULER UN PATIN: verbal expression. Here is the probable origin of the idiomatic expression "*rouler un patin*"—literally "to roll a skate"—and what we call the "French kiss." If you can figure out the connection, you're much brighter than I am! The slang expression "*rouler une galoche*" is used in a similar sense. The skate was first designed as a lady's shoe with thick soles that the stylish used to make themselves look taller. It was specially designed for a wooden-soled shoe in which the nails were modified with an iron blade for ice skating (1427). By comparison with the ice blade, it designated (around 1845) a metallic sole mounted on wheels, called (after 1868) a roller skate (*patin à roulettes*). This was probably the origin of the deep kiss (baiser profond): that is, the "*patin*." Would this then be a literal reference to sliding one's tongue in?

SMAC: noun, masculine. A kiss with a loud sound. From the English word "smack." Often seen in comic books—which the French adore!

SUÇON: noun, masculine. A hicky, a lovebite, a light bruise produced by kissing and sucking hard on the skin. Put your lips on your partner's skin, preferably on the neck, and take a long breath in. The goal of this vampire-like act is to leave the signature of the kiss on one's prey, a technique as old as mankind.

Dictionary of Foreign "Tongues"

How do you say, "May I kiss you" in a romantic context in different languages?

FRENCH: *"Puis-je me permettre de vous embrasser?"* is an extremely polite way of formulating your request. If you want to go right to the heart of the matter, say: *"Embrasse-moi!"*

GERMAN: *"Darf ich Sie küssen?"* You pronounce it while making a big smile as you pronounce the "ch" of ich while putting the tip of your tongue behind the lower teeth, against the gums. You will have every opportunity, in spite of grimacing, to be understood and to make someone laugh. And as folk wisdom has it: "Once you have made someone laugh, the rest is all..."

ITALIAN: *"Posso baciarti?"* among young people, and *"Potrei baciarla?"* more polite, formal.

PICARD: *"Donne un tcho bec à tun Quinquin!"* Picard is also known as Ch'timi, a dialect still spoken in Northern France.

RUSSIAN: Don't ask! Custom requires that you kiss each other on the mouth anyway.

SPANISH: *"¿Puedo besarle?"* (It's pronounced just like that!)

SWISS GERMAN: *"Chönnt'i dir ächt äs müntschi gää?"* Considered very charming with an English, American, or French accent. So that you formulate the question politely in Swiss German, you have to add *"ächt"* in the middle of the sentence, which means "perhaps." Something like: "Could I kiss you?"

"Happy end..."

Illustrations: Isabelle Chemin

ISBN : 2-84096-257-8
Dépôt légal : décembre 2001

Achevé d'imprimer en décembre 2001,
sur système Variquik
dans les ateliers de la Sagim, à Courtry
N° d'impression : 5530